THIS IS THE SPIRITUAL LIFE

*Orthodox Spirituality According to
the Alexandrian Fathers*

FR. D. ABBA MOSES

This is the Spiritual Life: Orthodox Spirituality According to the Alexandrian Fathers
By Fr. D. Abba Moses

Copyright © 2025 Coptic Orthodox Diocese of the Southern U.S.A.

All rights reserved.

Designed & Published by:
St. Mary & St. Moses Abbey Press
101 S Vista Dr, Sandia, TX 78383
stmabbeypress.com

Cover photo is taken in St. Mary and St. Moses Abbey by one of the monks. The dove in the photo is not an added graphic, but a real dove.

Contents

This is the Spiritual Life 5
Illustrations 84
Bibliography 97

This is the Spiritual Life

Patristic Definition of the "Spiritual Life"

"By striving with all our might to do whatever is good and by setting our mind above the pleasures of the flesh, we may preserve intact the beauty of the image that is implanted in us.[1] This is the spiritual life, and this is the meaning of worship in the Spirit.[2]"[3]

The Defined Goal: Preserving the image and likeness of God that has been implanted in us.

The Two Means Mentioned:
1. Think good
2. Do good

In the Alexandrian Tradition, Image and Likeness Mean the Same Thing

"For God (…) made, through His own Word our Savior Jesus Christ, the human race after His own

---

1 ἐφέσει τῇ πρὸς πᾶν ὁτιοῦν ἀγαθὸν ὁλοσχερῶς ἀνακείμενο καὶ φιλοσαρκίας κρείττονα τὴν διάνοιαν ἔχοντες, ἀπαραποίητον ἐν ἑαυτοῖς τῆς ἐντεθείσης εἰκόνος τὸ κάλλος τηρήσωμεν

2 Οὗτος γὰρ ὁ βίος ὁ πνευματικὰς, αὕτη τῆς ἐν Πνεύματι λατρείας ἡ δύναμις

3 Cyril of Alexandria. (2013–2015). *Commentary on John*. (J. C. Elowsky, T. C. Oden, & G. L. Bray, Eds., D. R. Maxwell, Trans.) (Vol. 2, p. 297). Downers Grove, IL: IVP Academic: An Imprint of InterVarsity Press. [Henceforth, Cyril, Commentary on John, Vol. 2, IVP Academic, 297].

image,[4] and constituted man able to see and know realities by means of this likeness to Himself[5]."[6]

"If they assert, 'in [God's] image,' and, 'in [God's] likeness' to be different things, they must explain the distinction. Our attitude is that 'image' means nothing other than 'likeness' and similarly 'likeness' nothing other than 'image.'[7]"[8]

Human Beings were Initially Created in God's Image and Likeness

"The Word of the Father after Whose likeness they [humans] were originally made.[9] For the soul is made after the image and likeness of God[10]."[11]

---

4 τὸ ἀνθρώπινον γένος κατ' ἰδίαν εἰκόνα πεποίηκε

5 Καὶ τῶν ὄντων αὐτὸν θεωρητὴν καὶ ἐπιστήμονα διὰ τῆς πρὸς αὐτὸν ὁμοιώσεως κατεσκεύασε

6 Athanasius of Alexandria. (1892). *Against the Heathen*. In P. Schaff & H. Wace (Eds.), & A. T. Robertson (Trans.), *St. Athanasius: Select Works and Letters* (Vol. 4, p. 5). Christian Literature Company. [Henceforth, Athanasius, Against the Heathen 2, (NPNF² 4), 5].

7 Διακείμεθα γὰρ ἡμεῖς, ὡς οὐδὲν ἕτερον τό, κατ' εἰκόνα δηλοῖ, πλὴν ὅτι, καθ' ὁμοίωσιν, καὶ ὁμοίως τὸ, καθ' ὁμοίωσιν, τῷ, κατ' εἰκόνα

8 Cyril of Alexandria. (1983). *Doctrinal Questions and Answers*. L. Wickham (Trans.), *Cyril of Alexandria: Select letters* (p. 193). Oxford: Oxford University Press.

9 καθ' ὃν καὶ γεγόνασιν ἐξ ἀρχῆς

10 Κατ' εἰκόνα γὰρ Θεοῦ πεποίηται, καὶ καθ' ὁμοίωσιν γέγονεν

11 Athanasius, Against the Heathen 34, (NPNF² 4), 22.

"So our forefather Adam was made, according to the faith contained in the sacred Scriptures, in the image and likeness of God[12],[13]"[14]

Being in God's Image and Likeness Means Possessing Some Divine Attributes

"For you know yourselves, and no one can dispute it, that 'like' is not based on essence, but on properties,[15] and qualities[16];[17] for in the case of essences we speak, not of likeness, but of identity. Man, for instance, is said to be like man, not in essence, but according to property[18] and character;[19] for in essence men are of one nature. And again, man is not said to be unlike

---

12 Πεποίηται τοίνυν ὁ προπά τωρ Αδάμ κατά γε τὴν πίστιν τῶν ἱερῶν Γραμμά των, κατ' εἰκόνα καὶ καθ' ὁμοίωσιν Θεοῦ.

13 Cf. Gn 1:26–27; 5:1.

14 St. Cyril of Alexandria. (2018-2019). *Glaphyra on the Pentateuch: Genesis, Exodus through Deuteronomy* (N. P. Lunn, Trans.; Vol. 1, p. 70). The Catholic University of America Press.

15 Σχημάτων (plural); σχῆμα: "character, characteristic property of a thing;" Liddell, H. G., Scott, R., Jones, H. S., & McKenzie, R. (1996). In *A Greek-English lexicon* (p. 1745). Clarendon Press. [Henceforth, Liddell, p. 1745].

16 Ποιοτήτων (plural); ποιότης: "quality;" Liddell, p. 1431.

17 τὸ ὅμοιον οὐκ ἐπὶ τῶν οὐσιῶν, ἀλλ' ἐπὶ σχημάτων καὶ ποιοτήτων λέγεται ὅμοιον

18 σχῆμα: "character, characteristic property of a thing;" Liddell, p. 1745.

19 Ανθρωπος γοῦν ἀνθρώπῳ ὅμοιος λέγεται, οὐ κατὰ τὴν οὐσίαν, ἀλλὰ κατὰ τὸ σχῆμα καὶ τὸν χαρακτῆρα

dog, but to be of different nature. Accordingly while the former are of one nature and coessential, the latter are different in both."[20]

"Or rather let us anticipate their argument and with apt reasoning spell out beforehand the kinds of images there are. In this way, the results of our investigation will be clear and crisp. The first kind of image is characterized by identity of nature in identical properties,[21] like Abel from Adam or Isaac from Abraham. The second consists only in the likeness of imprint and the precise representation of the form, like the picture of a king on wood,[22] or made in some other way, representing him as excellently and skillfully as possible. Another kind of image is taken to refer to habits, manners, way of life and inclination toward things that are good or bad,[23] as for example when one says that someone who does good is like Paul and someone who does not is like Cain. The fact that they are equally good or bad brings about and reasonably confers a likeness with each one.[24] Another kind of

---

20 Athanasius, Councils of Ariminum and Seleucia 53, (NPNF² 4), 478–479.

21 Ουκουν μια μεν ηδη και πρωτη της κατά φυσιν ταυτοτητος εν απαραλλακτοις τοις ιδιωμασιν η εικων

22 Δευτερα δε παλιν η κατά μονην την του χαρακτηρος εμφερειαν, και το ακριβες του ειδους εκτυπωμα, καθαπερ η του βασιλεως εν ξυλω γραφυ

23 Εικων δε ετερα λαμβανεται παλιν προς ηθη, και τροπους, και πολιτειαν, και θελημα το επι τισιν αγαθοις η φαυλοις

24 Το γαρ εν τοις ισοις ορασθαι φαυλοις το και αγαθοις, την ομοιωσιν εκαστω πραγματευεται και περιτιθησιν εικοτως

image is that of dignity, honor, glory and excellence,[25] as for example if someone were to succeed another in command and do with authority everything that is proper and fitting for the predecessor. In another sense, an image concerns some other quality or quantity of a thing, its shape and proportion[26] (for we must keep it short)."[27]

"In applying to man the being formed into the divine image,[28] we said that man was made in the likeness of his Creator in terms of the quality of his characteristics,[29] habits[30] and the spiritual shape which appears through the beauty of virtues.[31]"[32]

---

25 Ειδος δε πως εικονος εστιν ετερον, και το εν αξιωματι, και τιμη, και δοξη, και υπεροχη

26 Εικων δε ετερως, η καθ' ετεραν πιοιτητα πραγματος, η ποσοτητα, σχημα τε και αναλογιαν

27 Cyril, Commentary on John, Vol. 1, IVP Academic, 152–153.

28 ἐξεικονισμόν; ἐξεικονίζω: "formed in the image of;" Liddell, p. 589.

29 ἠθῶν; ἦθος: "disposition, character (...) moral character (...) traits, characteristics;" Liddell, p. 766.

30 Τρόπων; τρόπος: "of persons, a way of life, habit, custom (...) a man's ways, habits, character, temper;" Liddell, p. 1827.

31 Εφαρμόζοντες δὲ τῷ ἀνθρώπῳ τὸν θεῖον ἐξεικονισμόν, ἐλέγομεν ὅτι κατὰ τὴν τῶν ἠθῶν ἤτοι τῶν τρόπων ποιότητα, καὶ κατ' εἶδος τὸ πνευματικὸν, ὃ διὰ τῆς εὐειδίας τῶν δἀρετῶν ἐκφαίνεται, πεποιῆσθαι καθ' ὁμοίωσιν αὐτοῦ τοῦ Δημιουργοῦ

32 Cyril of Alexandria. (1983). *Answers to Tiberius*. L. Wickham (Trans.), *Cyril of Alexandria: Select letters* (p. 175). Oxford: Oxford University Press.

Specific Examples Include:

1. Rationality

"But that what came into being might not only be, but be good,[33] it pleased God that His own Wisdom should condescend[34] to the creatures, so as to introduce an impress and appearance of Its Image on all in common and on each, that what was made might be manifestly wise works and worthy of God. For as of the Son of God, considered as the Word,[35] our word is an image, so of the same Son considered as Wisdom is the wisdom which is implanted in us an image;[36] in which wisdom we, having the power of knowledge and thought, become recipients of the All-framing Wisdom; and through It we are able to know Its Father."[37]

"The fact that man was made according to the image of God[38] has different meanings and insinuations.[39] Man,

---

33 Ἵνα δὲ μὴ μόνον ὑπάρχῃ τὰ γενόμενα ἀλλὰ καὶ καλῶς ὑπάρχῃ

34 συγκαταβῆναι

35 Λογος: "inward debate of the soul (...) thinking, reasoning (...) reflection, deliberation (...) in idea, in thought (...) reasoning convinces (...) scientific knowledge and right process of thought;" Liddell, p. 1058.

36 εἰκών ἐστιν ὁ ἡμέτερος λόγος, οὕτως ὄντος αὐτοῦ Σοφίας εἰκὼν πάλιν ἐστὶνή ἐν ἡμῖν γενομένη σοφία

37 Athanasius, *Four Discourses against the Arians* II.XXII.78, (NPNF² 4), 390.

38 Cf. Gn 1:26.

39 Τὸ δὲ κατ' εἰκόνα Θεοῦ τὸν ἄνθρωπον πεποιῆσθαι, ἑτέρας ἐμφάσεις καὶ ὑπονοίας ἔχει

alone among all the living creatures on the earth, is rational, compassionate, has an inclination[40] toward every virtue, and has assigned to him rule over all things upon the earth, in "the image and likeness" of God.[41] Accordingly, as man is a rational, living being, and insofar as he loves virtue, and has power over the things on earth, it is stated that he has been made in the image of God[42]."[43]

2. Wisdom

"'The Lord created me for His works;' for what the wisdom in us says, that the Lord Himself speaks as if it were His own; and, whereas He is not Himself created, being Creator, yet because of the image of Him created in the works,[44] He says this as if of Himself."[45]

"Do you therefore ask the bestowal without limitation of spiritual gifts. Ask strength, that you may be able manfully to resist every fleshly lust. Ask of God

---

40 ἐπιτηδειότητα; ἐπιτηδειότης: "fitness, suitableness, convenience for a purpose (...) tendency, liability (...) potentiality, capacity;" Liddell, p. 666.
41 μόνος γὰρ αὐτὲς παρὰ πάντα τὰ ἐπὶ τῆς γῆς ζῶα λογικός ἐστι, φιλοικτείρμων, ἐπιτηδειότητα πρὸς πᾶσαν ἔχων ἀρετὴν, λαχών δὲ καὶ τὸ ἄρχειν ἁπάντων τῶν ἐπὶ τῆς γῆς, καθ' ὁμοιότητα καὶ εἰκόνα Θεοῦ
42 Ουκουν κατά το εινα ζωον λογικον και καθο φιλαρετον και αρχικον των επι της γης
43 Cyril of Alexandria. (1987). *Letters, 51–110* (T. P. Halton, Ed.; J. I. McEnerney, Trans.; Vol. 77, p. 110). The Catholic University of America Press.
44 ιὰ δὲ τὴν ἐν τοῖς ἔργοις εἰκόνα κτισθεῖσαν αὐτοῦ
45 Athanasius, Four Discourses against the Arians II.XXII.78, (NPNF² 4), 390–391.

an uncovetous disposition; long suffering; gentleness; and the mother and nurse of all good, I mean, patience. Ask calmness of temper; self-control; a pure heart; and further, ask also the wisdom that comes from Him. These things He will give readily: these save the soul: these work in it that better beauty, and imprint in it God's image."[46]

3. Free-will

"In the beginning man was made with control over his own will and with a disposition that was free to do whatever he chose, for the Deity, in whose likeness he was formed, is free."[47]

"Rather, after the creature was ensouled, or rather after it arrived at the condition of its complete nature through both (I mean soul and body), then, like a stamp of His own nature, the Creator fixed upon it the Holy Spirit, that is, the Breath of Life, through which He shaped it into Its archetypal beauty.[48] It was completed in the image of its Creator and made constant in every form of virtue by the power of the

---

46 Cyril of Alexandria. (1859). *A Commentary upon the Gospel according to S. Luke* (R. P. Smith, Trans.; p. 361). Oxford University Press. [Henceforth, Cyril, Commentary on Luke, 361].

47 St. Cyril of Alexandria. (2018-2019). *Glaphyra on the Pentateuch: Genesis, Exodus through Deuteronomy* (N. P. Lunn, Trans.; Vol. 1, p. 59). The Catholic University of America Press.

48 Ψυχωθεντι δε μαλλον και προς ιδιοτητα της τελειας φυσεως δι' αμφοιν αφιγμενω, ψυχης δη λεγω και σωματος, καθαπερ τινα σφραγιδα της εαυτου φυσεως εωεπηξεν ο Δυμιουργος το Πνευμα το αγιον, τουτ' εστι, την πνοην της ζωης, δι' ης προς το αρχετυπον διεπλαττετο καλλος

Holy Spirit, who dwelt in it.[49] But since it was capable of free choice and entrusted with the reins of its own will—that too is part of the image, since God has control over His own will[50]—it turned and fell."[51]

4. Goodness, Holiness or Righteousness

"For man upon earth, as far as his bodily nature is concerned, is dust and ashes: but he has been honored by God, by having been made in His image and likeness: not in his bodily shape, that is, but rather because he is capable of being just and good, and fitted for all virtue."[52]

"Man on the other hand, we say, was created, 'on earth in God's image,' because he is capable of being righteous, holy, good and wise."[53]

5. Freedom (from Servanthood)

"After all, He cannot bestow the honor of freedom on others if His own nature is bereft of it. I maintain that He must have this more than the others, since He is going to give His own good Quality (freedom) to those

---

49 Απετελειτο δε κατ' εικονα του Κτισαντος, προς πασαν ιδεαν αρετης δυναμει του ενοικισθεντος αυτω διακρατουμενος
50 Επειδη δε αυτοπροαιρετος ων, και τας των ιδιων θεληματων πεπιστευμενος ηνιας (μοιρα γαρ της εικονος και αυτή κατεξουσιαζει γαρ των οικειων θεληματων Θεος)
51 Cyril, Commentary on John, Vol. 2, IVP Academic, 187–188.
52 Cyril, Commentary on Luke, 446.
53 Cyril of Alexandria. (1983). *Answers to Tiberius*. L. Wickham (Trans.), *Cyril of Alexandria: Select letters* (p. 139). Oxford: Oxford University Press.

who do not have it.⁵⁴ But as for the holy Apostles and all others who ascend by faith to friendship with our Lord Jesus Christ, this dignity would be given and imparted from the outside, as an honor, not in the same way as His dignity. They who mount up to the glory of freedom by likeness to Him would display something that belongs naturally to Him and Him alone⁵⁵."⁵⁶

6. Sonship (Adoption)

"Therefore, in speaking of 'like' according to essence, we mean like from participation;⁵⁷ for 'likeness' is a quality, which may attach⁵⁸ to essence,⁵⁹ and this would be proper to creatures, for they, by partaking, are made like God.⁶⁰ For 'when He shall appear,' says Scripture, 'we shall be like Him, '⁶¹ like, that is, not in essence but in sonship, which we shall partake from Him⁶²."⁶³

---

54 Δώσει γὰρ τότε πρεπωδέστερον τοῖς οὐκ ἔχουσι τὸ ἴδιον ἀγαθόν

55 Οἱ γὰρ τῇ πρὸς αὐτὸν ὁμοιώσει πρὸς τὴν τῆς ἐλευθερίας ἀνατρέχοντες δόξαν, αὐτῷ δὴ τούτῳ καὶ μόνῳ προσὸν φυσικῶς ἀποδείξειαν

56 Cyril, Commentary on John, Vol. 2, IVP Academic, 232.

57 Διὸ καὶ ὁ λέγων ὅμοιον κατ' οὐσίαν ἐκ μετουσίας τοῦ το λέγει ὅμοιον

58 προσγένοιτ'; προσγίγνομαι: "attach oneself to another (...) to be added, accrue;" Liddell, p. 1505.

59 Τὸ γὰρ ὅμοιον ποιότης ἐστίν, ἥτις τῇ οὐσίᾳ προσγένοιτ' ἄν

60 ταῦτα γὰρ ἐκ μετοχῆς ὁμοιοῦται τῷ Θεῷ

61 1 John 3:2

62 ὅμοιοι δηλονότι οὐ τῇ οὐσίᾳ ἀλλὰ τῇ υἱότητι, ἧς μεταλαμβάνομεν παρ' αὐτοῦ

63 Athanasius, Councils of Ariminum and Seleucia 53,

"He wore the form of a slave, even though He was by nature Lord and Son, that He might transfer what is a slave by nature into the glory of sonship, in conformity with His own likeness, like Him.[64] Since He became like us (that is, a human being) in order that we might become like Him (I mean gods and sons), He receives the things [attributes] that are properly ours into Himself and He gives us the Things that are His own in return[65] (…) We ascend to honors above our nature by our likeness to Him,[66] for though we are not sons by nature, we are called sons of God."[67]

7. Authority

"The fact that man was made according to the image of God[68] has different meanings and insinuations.[69] Man, alone among all the living creatures on the earth, is rational, compassionate, has an inclination[70] toward

---

(NPNF² 4), 478–479.

64 Ινα το τη φυσει δουλον εις την της υιοθεσιας μετακομιση δοξαν, καθ' ομοιοτητα την εαυτου, και ως προς αυτον

65 Ως ουν καθ' ημας γεγονως, τουτ' εστιν ανθρωπος, ινα και ημεις κατ' αυτόν [γενωμεθα], φημι δη θεοι και υιοι, δεχαται μεν εις εαυτον τα ημων ιδικως, αντιδιδωσι δε ημιν τα εαυτου

66 Ιν' ωσπερ ημεις εις το υπερ φυσιν αξιωμα δια της προς αυτόν ομοιωσεως αναβαινομεν

67 Cyril, Commentary on John, Vol. 2, IVP Academic, 363.

68 Cf. Gn 1:26.

69 Τὸ δὲ κατ' εἰκόνα Θεοῦ τὸν ἄνθρωπον πεποιῆσθαι, ἑτέρας ἐμφάσεις καὶ ὑπονοίας ἔχει

70 ἐπιτηδειότητα; ἐπιτηδειότης: "fitness, suitableness, convenience for a purpose (…) tendency, liability (…) potentiality, capacity;" Liddell, p. 666.

every virtue, and has assigned to him rule over all things upon the earth, in 'the image and likeness' of God.[71] Accordingly, as man is a rational, living being, and insofar as he loves virtue, and has power over the things on earth, it is stated that he has been made in the image of God[72]."[73]

"There are good grounds too for saying that the likeness to God existed in man at the beginning, because it has been given to man to rule the inhabitants of the earth.[74] This is a second explanation of the likeness to God[75]."[76]

8. *Incorruption or indestructibility*

"So the Word of God came Himself, in order that He being the Image of the Father,[77] the human being 'in

---

71 μόνος γὰρ αὐτὲς παρὰ πάντα τὰ ἐπὶ τῆς γῆς ζῶα λογικός ἐστι, φιλοικτείρμων, ἐπιτηδειότητα πρὸς πᾶσαν ἔχων ἀρετὴν, λαχὼν δὲ καὶ τὸ ἄρχειν ἁπάντων τῶν ἐπὶ τῆς γῆς, καθ' ὁμοιότητα καὶ εἰκόνα Θεοῦ

72 Ουκουν κατά το εινα ζωον λογικον και καθο φιλαρετον και αρχικον των επι της γης

73 Cyril of Alexandria. (1987). *Letters, 51-110.* (T. P. Halton, Ed.; J. I. McEnerney, Trans.; p. 110). The Catholic University of America Press.

74 Οὐκ ἀπίθανον δὲ καὶ κατὰ τὸ ἀρχικὸν ἐνεῖναι λέγειν τῷ ἀνθρώπῳ τὴν ὁμοίωσιν τὴν πρὸς Θεόν. Δέδοται γὰρ αὐτῷ τὸ ἄρχειν ἁπάντων τῶν ἐπὶ τῆς γῆς

75 δεύτερος οὗτος τῆς πρὸς αὐτὸν ὁμοιώσεως λόγος

76 Cyril of Alexandria. (1983). *Answers to Tiberius.* L. Wickham (Trans.), *Cyril of Alexandria: Select letters* (pp. 165-167). Oxford: Oxford University Press.

77 Cf. Col 1:15.

the image' might be recreated[78].[79] It [being recreated 'in the image'] could not, again, have been done in any other way, without death and corruption being utterly destroyed.[80] So He rightly took a mortal body,[81] that in It death might henceforth be destroyed utterly and human beings be renewed[82] again according to the image[83]."[84]

"And now my discussion may be more involved than is necessary, but it must nevertheless proceed and show what our original condition[85] was. I think a sincere desire to grasp the meaning will be completely free of the sins that arise from sluggishness. So this rational earthly animal, I mean the human being, was created from the beginning 'in the image of the Creator,'[86] according to the Scriptures. And there are different meanings of 'image.'[87] There are not one but many kinds of images.[88] However, the element of

---

78   ἀνακτίσαι

79   τὸν κατ' εἰκόνα ἄνθρωπον ἀνακτίσαι δυνηθῇ

80   μὴ ὁ θάνατος ἦν καὶ ἡ φθορὰ ἐξαφανισθεῖσα

81   Ὅθεν εἰκότως ἔλαβε σῶμα θνητόν

82   ἀνακαινισθῶσιν; ἀνακαινόω: "to be renewed;" Liddell, p. 107.

83   ὁ θάνατος ἐν αὐτῷ λοιπὸν ἐξαφανισθῆναι δυνηθῇ, καὶ οἱ κατ' εἰκόνα πάλιν ἀνακαινισθῶσιν ἄνθρωποι

84   St. Athanasius the Great of Alexandria. (2011). *On the Incarnation: Translation* (J. Behr, Ed. & Trans.; p. 79). SVS Press.

85   Ημας αρχαιοτητα

86   ἐξ ἀρχῆς, κατ' εἰκόνα τοῦ Κτίσαντος

87   Καὶ διάφορος μὲν της εικονος ο λογος

88   Εικων γαρ ου καθ' ένα τροπον, αλλα κατά πολλους

likeness[89] to God the Creator that is most manifest of all is incorruptibility and indestructibility[90]."[91]

9. Immortality

"So the Word of God came Himself, in order that He being the Image of the Father,[92] the human being 'in the image' might be recreated[93].[94] It [being recreated 'in the image'] could not, again, have been done in any other way, without death and corruption being utterly destroyed.[95] So He rightly took a mortal body,[96] that in It death might henceforth be destroyed utterly and human beings be renewed[97] again according to the image[98]."[99]

"What again that [image] of the heavenly [man]? being in no way overcome by [sinful] passions, not knowing transgression, not being subject to death and

---

89 Εμφερειας; ἐμφέρεια: "likeness;" Liddell, p. 550.

90 Μερος γε μην το των αλλων μαλιστα διαφανεστατον της προς τον ποιησαντα Θεον εμφερειας, το αφθαρτον και ανωλεθρον

91 Cyril, Commentary on John, Vol. 2, IVP Academic, 187.

92 Cf. Col 1:15.

93 ἀνακτίσαι

94 τὸν κατ' εἰκόνα ἄνθρωπον ἀνακτίσαι δυνηθῇ

95 μὴ ὁ θάνατος ἦν καὶ ἡ φθορὰ ἐξαφανισθεῖσα

96 Ὅθεν εἰκότως ἔλαβε σῶμα θνητόν

97 ἀνακαινισθῶσιν; ἀνακαινόω: "to be renewed;" Liddell, p. 107.

98 ὁ θάνατος ἐν αὐτῷ λοιπὸν ἐξαφανισθῆναι δυνηθῇ, καὶ οἱ κατ' εἰκόνα πάλιν ἀνακαινισθῶσιν ἄνθρωποι

99 St. Athanasius the Great of Alexandria. (2011). *On the Incarnation: Translation* (J. Behr, Ed. & Trans.; p. 79). SVS Press.

decay, holiness, righteousness, and whatever are akin to and like these[100]."[101]

10. Godhood[102]

"For therefore did He assume the Body originate and human, that having renewed[103] It as Its Framer, He might deify It in Himself, and thus might introduce us all into the kingdom of Heaven after His likeness.[104] For man had not been deified if joined to a creature,[105] or unless the Son were true God."[106]

"When we are formed to be like Him through participation in[107] the Spirit, then we are called

---

100 τὸ κατ' οὐδένα τρόπον ἡττᾶσθαι παθῶν ·τὸ μὴ εἰδέναι πλημελεῖν·τὸ μὴ ὑποκεῖσθαι θανάτῳ καὶ φθορᾷ· ὁ ἁγιασμός, ἡ δικαιοσύνη · καὶ ὅσα τούτοις ἀδελφά τε καὶ παραπλήσια

101 Cyril of Alexandria. (1881). *Five Tomes against Nestorius; Scholia on the Incarnation; Christ Is One; Fragments against Diodore of Tarsus, Theodore of Mopsuestia, the Synousiasts* (pp. 94–95). James Parker and Co.; Rivingtons.

102 This only means being made into a god by grace and not by becoming constituted or made of the Divine Essence.

103 ἀνακαινίσας

104 ἐν ἑαυτῷ θεοποιήσῃ, καὶ οὕτως εἰς βασιλείαν οὐρανῶν εἰσαγάγῃ πάντας ἡμᾶς καθ' ὁμοιότητα ἐκείνου

105 Οὐκ ἂν δὲ πάλιν ἐθεοποιήθη κτίσματι συναφθεὶς ὁ ἄνθρωπος

106 Athanasius, Four Discourses against the Arians II.XXI.70, (NPNF² 4), 386.

107 This phrase "participation in" does not mean that we become constituted or made up of the Divine Essence; rather, it is synonymous of the phrase "partaking of," and means that the Divine Essence shares grace or gifts with us. The same holds true for all subsequent occurrences of the phrases

'children of God' and 'gods'[108]."[109]

Another Divine Attribute of Interest, Included in being in God's Image and Likeness, is Love

"The act [of love] is better than any other kind of well doing [virtue]: for it works in our souls a certain divine likeness which molds us, so to speak, after (into) God's image."[110]

"Therefore, the boast of love is the face and image of Christ the Savior in us[111]."[112]

Love can also be Called Purity of Heart

"Hence it is clearly proved that perfection is not immediately arrived at by being stripped and deprived of all one's wealth or by giving up one's honors, unless there is that love whose elements the Apostle describes, which consists in purity of heart alone. For what else does it mean not to be envious, not to be boastful, not to be angry, not to do evil, not to seek the things that are one's own, not to rejoice over iniquity, not to think evil and all the rest,[113] if

---

"participation in" and "participate in."
108 Προς ον και αυτοι μορφουμενοι δια μετουσιας του Πνευματος, και τεκνα Θεου και θεοι χρηματιζομεν
109 Cyril, Commentary on John, Vol. 2, IVP Academic, 285.
110 Cyril, Commentary on Luke, 531–532.
111 Πρόσωπον οὖν ἄρα, καὶ εἰκὼν ἐν ἡμῖν τοῦ Σωτῆρος Χριστοῦ, τῆς ἀγάπης τὸ καύχημα
112 Cyril, Commentary on John, Vol. 2, IVP Academic, 141.
113 Cf. 1 Cor 13:4–7.

not always to offer God a perfect and utterly clean heart and to keep it unsullied by any passion?"[114]

So it is also Correct to Say that Love, or Purity of Heart, is a Goal of the Spiritual Life

"So the soul too, turning from the way toward God, and driving the members of the body beyond what is proper, or rather, driven herself along with them by her own doing, sins and makes evil for herself, not seeing that she has strayed from the way, and has swerved from the goal of truth, to which the Christ-bearing man, the blessed Paul, was looking when he said, "I press on toward the goal unto the prize of the high calling of Christ Jesus[115]:" so that the holy man, making goodness[116] his mark,[117] never did what was evil."[118]

"Since God observes, then, and carefully scrutinizes all our affairs, truly good and prudent people should follow straight paths and consider nothing to be as important as love for God and brethren. Love for God involves a faith that is genuine and lasting, and love for the brethren is linked to the achievements of righteousness."[119]

---

114 John Cassian. (1997). *John Cassian: The Conferences* (W. J. Burghardt, J. Dillon, & D. D. McManus, Eds.; B. Ramsey, Trans.; Vol. 57, p. 45). Newman Press. [Henceforth, Cassian, The Conferences, 45].

115 Phil. 3:14.

116 John 14:21 & 23.

117 σκοπῶν γοῦν τὸ καλὸν

118 Athanasius, Against the Heathen 5, (NPNF² 4), 6.

119 Cyril of Alexandria. (2008). *Commentary on the Twelve*

"It is our duty therefore to be faithful unto God, pure in heart, merciful and kind, just and holy."[120]

"The end of our profession, as we have said, is the kingdom of God or the kingdom of heaven; but the [immediate] goal or scopos[121] is purity of heart, without which it is impossible for anyone to reach that end."[122]

The Monastic Fathers taught that purity of heart, or love, which is part of being in God's image and likeness, is to be one's goal.

"For the sake of the principal scopos [goal], which is purity of heart or love."[123]

Thus, both the Patristic and Monastic Fathers agree and have consensus on what the goal of the spiritual life is.

Partaking or Participation is the Process by which We Receive Some Divine Attributes which the Holy Trinity Shares with Us

"All things originated have by participation the Grace of God[124]."[125]

Prophets (T. P. Halton, Ed.; R. C. Hill, Trans.; Vol. 116, p. 109). The Catholic University of America Press.

120 Cyril, Commentary on Luke, 514.
121 Σκοπός: "mark or object on which one fixes the eye (...) aim, end, object;" Liddell, p. 1614.
122 Cassian, The Conferences, 43.
123 Cassian, The Conferences, 45–46.
124 τὰ μὲν γενητὰ πάντα ἐκ μετουσίας ἔχει τὴν παρὰ Θεοῦ χάριν
125 Athanasius, Councils of Ariminum and Seleucia 51, (NPNF[2] 4), 477.

"For you know yourselves, and no one can dispute it, that 'like' is not based on essence, but on properties,[126] and qualities[127];[128] for in the case of essences we speak, not of likeness, but of identity. Man, for instance, is said to be like man, not in essence, but according to property[129] and character;[130] for in essence men are of one nature. (...) Therefore, in speaking of 'like' according to essence, we mean like from participation;[131] for 'likeness' is a quality, which may attach[132] to essence,[133] and this would be proper to creatures, for they, by partaking, are made like God.[134] For 'when He shall appear,' says Scripture, 'we shall be like Him,'[135] like, that is, not in essence but in sonship, which we shall partake from Him[136]."[137]

---

126 Σχημάτων (plural); σχῆμα: "character, characteristic property of a thing;" Liddell, p. 1745.

127 Ποιοτήτων (plural); ποιότης: "quality;" Liddell, p. 1431.

128 τὸ ὅμοιον οὐκ ἐπὶ τῶν οὐσιῶν, ἀλλ' ἐπὶ σχημάτων καὶ ποιοτήτων λέγεται ὅμοιον

129 σχῆμα: "character, characteristic property of a thing;" Liddell, p. 1745.

130 Ανθρωπος γοῦν ἀνθρώπῳ ὅμοιος λέγεται, οὐ κατὰ τὴν οὐσίαν, ἀλλὰ κατὰ τὸ σχῆμα καὶ τὸν χαρακτῆρα

131 Διὸ καὶ ὁ λέγων ὅμοιον κατ' οὐσίαν ἐκ μετουσίας τοῦ το λέγει ὅμοιον

132 προσγένοιτ'; προσγίγνομαι: "attach oneself to another (...) to be added, accrue;" Liddell, p. 1505.

133 Τὸ γὰρ ὅμοιον ποιότης ἐστίν, ἥτις τῇ οὐσίᾳ προσγένοιτ' ἄν

134 ταῦτα γὰρ ἐκ μετοχῆς ὁμοιοῦται τῷ Θεῷ

135 1 John 3:2.

136 ὅμοιοι δηλονότι οὐ τῇ οὐσίᾳ ἀλλὰ τῇ υἱότητι, ἧς μεταλαμβάνομεν παρ' αὐτοῦ

137 Athanasius, Councils of Ariminum and Seleucia 53, (NPNF[2] 4), 478–479.

"Let Him be sanctified, it says, therefore—that is, let Him be considered or confessed to be holy. Now, this would be appropriate in God's case, and specifically and characteristically His alone;[138] even if there are many holy people and rational powers, including people on Earth, they are nevertheless made holy from participation in the One who is holy by nature, and who alone is truly called so. Just as it is He who is the true light, remember, but gave the privilege also to others, saying, 'You are the light of the world,' so too the One who alone is holy together with the God and Father and the Holy Spirit gives It, as from His fullness, to those sharing holiness with Him[139].[140]

"In the Nature that transcends all, even in God only, is found the Attribute of being by nature, and unchangeably good: but the angels, and we upon earth, are good by resembling Him, or rather by participation of Him. For as He is what He is, and this is His Name, and His everlasting memorial for all generations; but we exist and come into being by being made partakers of Him Who really exists: for God [is by] nature good and existing [by nature] as good is proper [to], essentially inherent [in] and an

---

138 Θεῷ δ'ἂν πρέποι τοῦτο, καὶ μόνῳ κυρίως τε καὶ ἰδικῶς

139 Οὕτω καὶ μόνος ὢν ἅγιος ὁμοῦ τῷ Θεῷ, καὶ Πατρί, καὶ τῷ ἁγίῳ Πνεύματι δίδωσιν ὡς ἐξ ἰδίου πληρώματος, καὶ τοῖς μετόχοις αὐτοῦ τὸν ἁγιασμόν

140 Cyril of Alexandria. (2008). *Commentary on Isaiah* (R. C. Hill, Trans.; Vol. 3, p. 201-202). Holy Cross Orthodox Press.

exclusively characteristic honor of Him; but we, and angels, [are good] according to participation[141]."[142]

When Adam and Eve Disobeyed God His Image and Likeness within Them was Lost[143]

"But if, once the transgression had taken off, human beings were now held fast in natural corruption[144] and were deprived[145] of the Grace of being in the image,[146] what else needed to happen?"[147]

"So when like a grain He fell into the ground, He was like an ear of wheat, but later He bore fruit, and human nature was refashioned in Him, brought back to the original image, to be just as the first man was[148]."[149]

---

141 Φύσει γὰρ ἀγαθὸς ὁ Θεός, καὶ ἴδιον αὐτοῦ καὶ οὐσιωδῶς ἐμπεφυκὸς καὶ ἐξαίρετον ἀξίωμα, τὸ εἶναι ἀγαθὸν, κατὰ μέθεξιν δὲ, ἄγγελοι καὶ ἡμεῖς

142 Cyril, Commentary on Luke, 566–567.

143 There are varying schools of thought on this point; they range from saying the image and likeness were damaged and corrupted to saying they were destroyed and lost.

144 τὴν κατὰ φύσιν φθορὰν

145 ἀφαιρεθέντες; ἀφαιρέω: "take away from (...) cancel or rescind (...) to be robbed or deprived of a thing;" Liddell, p. 286.

146 τὴν τοῦ κατ' εἰκόνα χάριν ἀφαιρεθέντες ἦσαν

147 St. Athanasius the Great of Alexandria. (2011). *On the Incarnation: Translation* (J. Behr, Ed. & Trans.; p. 65). SVS Press.

148 ἀναπλαττομένης ἐν αὐτῷ, πρὸς τὴν ἐν ἀρχαῖς εἰκόνα, καθ᾽ ἣν ὁ πρῶτος γέγονεν ἄνθρωπος

149 St. Cyril of Alexandria. (2018-2019). *Glaphyra on the Pentateuch: Genesis, Exodus through Deuteronomy* (N. P. Lunn,

"Truly it was especially fitting for the righteous Father to lift up what had been cast down by the devil's malice, and to restore to its original position what had been dragged off to where it should not be, and to free it from the foulness of sin and remold it to its original image, as it was created in the beginning.[150] It was also fitting for Him to subject him who crushed the image and irreverently dared to corrupt[151] it,[152] that is, Satan, to fitting punishment."[153]

"Man was made in His [God's] image in the beginning and his nature had an inclination[154] to acquiring[155] all good and successfully accomplishing virtue.[156] For He created us 'for good works' as all-

---

Trans.; Vol. 1, p. 75). The Catholic University of America Press.

150 Μεταπλασαι δε ωσπερ εις εικονα την πρωτην, το εν αρχαις ουτω πεποιημενον

151 Παραφθειραι; παραφθείρω: "destroy, corrupt, spoil (...) alter, corrupt;" Liddell, p. 1329.

152 Τον δε γε συντριψαντα και ανοσιως παραφθειραι τετολμηκοτα

153 Cyril, Commentary on John, Vol. 2, IVP Academic, 310.

154 ἐπιτηδείως; ἐπιτήδειος: "made for an end or purpose, fit or adapted for it, suitable, convenient (...) likely or inclined to come (...) requisite, necessaries (...) what is requisite, needful;" Liddell, p. 666.

155 ἀνάληψιν; ἀνάληψις: "taking up, e.g. suspension in a sling, fixing a bandage (...) acquirement of knowledge (...) assimilation;" Liddell, p. 111.

156 Γέγονε μὲν γὰρ κατ' εἰκόνα τὴν πρὸς αὐτὸν ἐν ἀρχαῖς ὁ ἄνθρωπος, καὶ ἡ φύσις ἦν ἔχουσα ἐπιτηδείως πρὸς ἀνάληψιν παντὸς ἀγαθοῦ, καὶ εἰς κατόρθωσιν ἀρετῆς

wise Paul writes. But sin destroyed[157] the beauty of the godlike[158] image and Satan made[159] the bright countenance[160] of humanity full of dirt[161,162]."[163]

God Wants His Image and Likeness to be Restored within Humans

"He also decreed to transform humanity once again into the original image through the Spirit.[164] There was no other way to make the divine imprint[165] shine again in humanity as it did at first."[166]

---

157 ἠφάνισεν; ἀφανίζω: "make unseen, hide (...) do away with, reject (...) make away with a person (...) in no part concealed or suppressed (...) do away with, remove (...) carry one off from the city (...) destroy (...) obliterate writing (...) obscure, mar one's good name (...) disguise it by dyeing (...) of artificial disfigurement (...) conceal the existence;" Liddell, p. 286.
158 θεοειδοῦς; θεοειδής: "godlike;" Liddell, p. 790.
159 ἀπέφηνεν; ἀποφαίνω: "render, make so and so;" Liddell, p. 225.
160 Πρόσωπον: "face, countenance (...) front, façade (...) one's look, countenance;" Liddell, p. 1533.
161 ῥυποῦ; ῥύπος: "dirt, filth;" Liddell, p. 1577.
162 Ἀλλὰ ἠφάνισεν τῆς θεοειδοῦς εἰκόνος τὸ κάλλος ἡ ἁμαρτία, καὶ ῥυποῦ μεστὸν τὸ λαμπρὸν τῆς ἀνθρωπότητος πρόσωπον ἀπέφηνεν ὁ Σατανᾶς
163 Cyril of Alexandria. (1983). *Answers to Tiberius*. L. Wickham (Trans.), *Cyril of Alexandria: Select letters* (p. 161). Oxford: Oxford University Press.
164 μεταστοιχειοῦν δὲ πάλιν εἰς τὴν ἀρχαίαν εἰκόνα τὴν ἀνθρωπότητα διὰ τοῦ Πνεύματος ἐδοκίμαζεν
165 θείους χαρακτῆρας
166 Cyril, Commentary on John, Vol. 1, IVP Academic, 82.

"He [God] desires, then, the nature of humanity to be renewed and reshaped into its original image by partaking of the Spirit[167] so that, by being clothed with that original grace and being restored [into] the shape [that is in conformity with] Him,[168] we may be found superior to and more powerful than sin, which reigns in this world, and we may devote ourselves only to the love of God."[169]

Striving for This Goal *Can*[170] Constitute Love

"The most wise Paul himself also testifies that love has created for itself a form of every virtue within the limits of itself and that it embraces in its arms, as it were, all that is good when he cries out, 'Love does not boast, it is not puffed up, it is not rude, it does not seek its own,'[171] and similar expressions"[172]

"You did not seek Me, He says, with pure motives, nor did you have a desire to excel in holiness. These are the things by which I would have known you. But

---

167 Ανανεουσθαι τοιγαρουν και αναπλαττεσθαι πως εις εικονα την πρωτην την ανθρωπου φυσιν ερωτα δια μετουσιας του Πνευματος

168 Την πρωτην εκεινην αμφεισαμενοι χαριν, και την προς αυτόν ανακομισαμενοι μορφωσιν

169 Cyril, Commentary on John, Vol. 2, IVP Academic, 297.

170 Because one's motive for preserving God's Image and Likeness determines if this is done out of love or not. See Isa 14:12–14 LXX.

171 1 Cor 13:4–5.

172 Cyril, Commentary on John, Vol. 2, IVP Academic, 140.

since you practiced a mere imaginary piety in order to seek gain, I justly declared that I did not know you."[173]

This love produced through the spiritual life will enable one to establish, maintain and grow in a personal relationship with the Holy Trinity.[174]

"So the person who chooses to live without love is not in God, instead lying outside of a relationship[175] with God[176]."[177]

"We interpret those who opt to adore[178] Him and Him alone, and follow the oracles given by Him, to be entering into an intimate relationship[179] with Him."[180]

---

173 Cyril, Commentary on John, Vol. 1, IVP Academic, 195.

174 Joh 10:14 & 1 Cor 8:3.

175 οἰκειότητος; οἰκειότης: "intimacy, friendship (...) living together as man and wife, domesticity, marriage;" Liddell, p. 1202.

176 Οὐκοῦν ὁ ἀγάπης δίχα διαζῆν ᾑρημένος, οὐκ ἐν τῷ Θεῷ πέποιθεν, ἀλλ' ἔξω κείσεται μᾶλλον τῆς πρὸς Θεὸν οἰκειότητος

177 Cyril of Alexandria. (2008). *Commentary on the Twelve Prophets* (T. P. Halton, Ed.; R. C. Hill, Trans.; Vol. 116, p. 25). The Catholic University of America Press.

178 προσκυνεῖν

179 οἰκειότητος; οἰκειότης: "kindred, relationship (...) intimacy, friendship (...) living together as man and wife, domesticity, marriage;" Liddell, p. 1202.

180 Cyril of Alexandria. (2012). *Commentary on the Twelve Prophets* (D. G. Hunter, Ed.; R. C. Hill, Trans.; Vol. 124, p. 22). The Catholic University of America Press.

Regaining or Restoration of That which was Lost is a Definition of Salvation

Greek Origin

σωτηρία: "deliverance, preservation."[181]

From σωτήρ: "savior, deliverer."[182]

From σώζω: "of things, keep safe, preserve (…) carry off safe, rescue from."[183]

From σῶς: "safe and **sound**,[184] alive and well, of persons (…) of things, safe, **whole**."[185]

Latin Origin

Salvare: "to save."

From salvus: "safe or uninjured." Uninjured means to be protected from damage. Damage means loss or harm caused by injury.

Salvation Occurs in Phases

Phase 1: Our Current Life on Earth

"He continues in obscure fashion to narrate that the outpouring of the Holy Spirit will be accorded the saints

---

181 Liddell, p. 1751.
182 Liddell, p. 1751.
183 Liddell, p. 1748.
184 "In good condition; not damaged, injured, or diseased."
185 Liddell, p. 1750.

in a most generous and abundant measure, especially at that time when they would be returned[186] to a holy and unending life—I mean, in the age to come.[187] You see, whereas at the present time we are enriched through faith in Christ with the first-fruits of the Holy Spirit by way of a pledge,[188] after our return from death to life[189] and the complete removal of sin it will not be by way of a pledge or measure that the divine Spirit will be in us. Instead, in a rich and abundant fashion, as I said, and in a perfect degree we shall by then luxuriate in His gifts through Christ. Hence His calling the Spirit living water, which He says will come out of the Jerusalem on high; since the inspired Scripture says the God of all dwells in Heaven, consequently the text says the life-giving Spirit will also come out from Heaven."[190]

"In this age[191] there is dire rebellion of the flesh, prompting the mind to improper pleasures, while the law of sin rages[192] in our limbs, even if it is overcome[193] by

---

186 ἀνακομισθεῖεν; ἀνακομίζω: "bring back, recover;" Liddell, p. 109.
187 καθ' ὃν ἂν εἰς ἁγίαν τε καὶ ἀείδρυτον ἀνακομισθεῖεν ζωήν, τὴν ὡς ἐν αἰῶνι, φημί, τῷ μέλλοντι
188 εἰς Χριστὸν ὡς ἐν ἀρραβῶνος τάξει τὴν ἀπαρχὴν τοῦ ἁγίου Πνεύματος πεπλουτήκαμεν
189 Μετὰ δέ γε τὴν ἐκ νεκρῶν ἀναβίωσιν
190 Cyril of Alexandria. (2012). *Commentary on the Twelve Prophets* (D. G. Hunter, Ed.; R. C. Hill, Trans.; Vol. 124, p. 264). The Catholic University of America Press.
191 τῷ αἰῶνι τούτῳ
192 ἀγριαίνει
193 νικᾶται

This is the Spiritual Life

the virtuousness[194] of the saints with Christ's assistance. Yet the mind is in some way intoxicated[195] and in a different way tested by the passions;[196] arrogance goes on the attack along with worldly vainglory, anger, avarice, and the other vices. Since we have been enriched with the pledge of the Spirit through Christ, however, we are accustomed to dominating the passions, though not without effort;[197] with the full light of the knowledge of God in the age to come, enriched with the perfection of the Gift of the Holy Spirit, and relieved of the corruption and passions of the flesh,[198] we shall serve God in every way, not half-hearted because of sin nor distracted by the passions of a former time, but living a pure and innocent life on a level with the holy angels."[199]

"Indeed, I have made you into gods and children of God—you who are human and who for this reason have the nature of a slave.[200] By grace I have made you illustrious with honor beyond your nature.[201] I have received you as sharers in My kingdom. I have

---

194 ἐπιεικείας

195 Καταμεθύει

196 Πειραζόμενος ὑπὸ παθῶν

197 εἰθίσμεθά τε κατευμεγεθεῖν τῶν παθῶν, πλὴν ἱρῶτος οὐ εἶχα

198 ἀποδυσάμενοί τε τήν φθοράν καὶ τὰ τῆς σαρκὸς πάθη

199 Cyril of Alexandria. (2012). *Commentary on the Twelve Prophets* (D. G. Hunter, Ed.; R. C. Hill, Trans.; Vol. 124, p. 341). The Catholic University of America Press.

200 Ανθρωπους γαρ οντας δουλην τε δια τουτο λαχοντας την φυσιν, θεους και υιους απεδειξα Θεου

201 Υπερ φυσιν

conformed you to the body of My glory.[202] I have honored you with incorruption and life.[203] All right, but these things are in hope and are reserved for the age to come.[204] What about the present age?[205] Have I not made you illustrious and glorious and made you respected[206] beyond all who love God? You have rebuked the unholy demons, and I have given you power to heal 'every disease and every sickness.'[207] I have promised you, 'Truly, truly I say to you, the one who believes in Me will also do the works that I do and, in fact, will do greater works than these'[208]."[209]

Complete Sinlessness is not Possible in this Age, but is Reserved for the Age to Come

"For there is no one free from defilement, though his course may have been but one hour on the Earth."[210]

"And this I know not how men endeavor to dispense with, saying of themselves that they are clean, and in their great madness not understanding, that to entertain such an idea of themselves is full of all

---

202 Phil 3:21.

203 Αφθαρσια τετιμηκα και ζωη

204 Αλλα ταυτα μεν εν ελπισι, και εις αιωνα τηρειται τον μελλοντα

205 Τι δε δη και εις το παρον;

206 Σεπτους; σεπτός: "august;" Liddell, p. 1591.

207 Mt 4:23.

208 Jn 14:12.

209 Cyril, Commentary on John, Vol. 2, IVP Academic, 228.

210 Athanasius, Festal Letters V.5, (NPNF[2] 4), 519.

impurity. For 'no man is free from defilement,'²¹¹ as it is written."²¹²

"For resting from wickedness is not yet entirely expelling wickedness.²¹³ The passions are often at rest in us.²¹⁴ They are not completely expelled from our mind, but by prudent reasoning they are led forcefully, as by a bridle, to an inactivity that is alien to them.²¹⁵ Yes, they yield against their will to the labors of asceticism.²¹⁶ But to shake off passion, insofar as a human can do this, is certainly something else besides this and far greater than resting from passions²¹⁷ (...) Resting from passions seems to lie somewhat within our powers (since we may cease from evil by inclining our will to the better), but being freed from passions is not at all in our powers; rather, that would be a work that is proper to Christ, who suffered for us in order to refashion everyone to newness of life.²¹⁸ Therefore,

---

211 Pro 20:9 LXX.
212 Cyril, Commentary on Luke, 700.
213 Το γαρ αργησαι φαθλοτητος, ουπω παντως εστι και φαθλοτητος αποβολη
214 Ηρεμει γαρ πολλακις εν ημιν τα παθη
215 Της μεν διανοιας ουκ εξωθεν οντα κατά το παντη. Λογισμω δε τω σωφρονι, καθαπερ τινι χαλινω, περιενεχθεντα βιαιως εις απαδουσαν αυτοις ησυχιαν
216 Τοις εις ασκησιν πονοις και ουχ εκοντα παραχωρειν
217 Το δε αποσεισασθαι παθος, οσον ανθρωπω πρεπει, παντως γε δηπου και ετερον τι παρ' εκεινο εστι, και πολύ τι μειζον παρα το αργησαι παθους
218 Αλλα το μεν αργησαι παθους, εχει τινα μοιραν του και εφ' ημιν κεισθαι δοκειν. Καταληξομεν γαρ του κακου τοις αμεινοσι των ιδιων θελημματων επιδιδοντες την ροπην. Το δε

circumcision was appropriately assigned the eighth day, the day of renewal, so to speak, because it ushers in the time of the resurrection, while rest received the seventh day, its neighbor that is a little behind. That is because rest, which is temporary and happens at will, falls a little short of the complete cutting off of passions."[219]

"The movement of the flesh fights against the mind longing for self-control through fear of God, and it puts up a terrible battle against purity.[220] Those, who make use of a sobriety appropriate for God-fearing people rebuke[221] the movement of the flesh, and by employing asceticism, hard work and other suitable aids dull the sting of sin.[222] Therefore it is impossible to uproot from the flesh its implanted[223] desire,[224] but,

---

απαλλαττεσθαι παθους, ουχι παντως εφ' ημιν, εργον δ' αν ειη πρεπον οντως Χριστω τω παθοντι υπερ ημων, ινα και παντα αναρρυθμιση προς καινιτητα ζωης

219 Cyril, Commentary on John, Vol. 1, IVP Academic, 288.

220 Καταστρατεύεται μὲν γὰρ τοῦ νοῦ βλέποντος εἰς ἐγκράτειαν διὰ τὸν φόβον τοῦ Θεοῦ τὸ κίνημα τῆς σαρκός, καὶ ταῖς εἰς ἁγνείαν ὁρμαῖς ἀντιτάττεται καὶ ἀντεξάγει δεινῶς

221 ἐπιτιμῶσι; ἐπιτιμάω: "object to one as blameable (...) rebuke, censure, of persons;" Liddell, p. 667.

222 'Ἀλλ' οἱ νήψει τῇ πρεπούσῃ χρώμενοι, τὸν Θεὸν σεβόμενοι, ἐπιτιμῶσι τῷ τῆς σαρκὸς κινήματι, καὶ τὸ τῆς ἁμαρτίας ἀμβλύνουσι κέντρον ἀσκήσει καὶ πόνοις, καὶ ταῖς ἄλλαις χρώμενοι ἐπιεικείαις

223 ἔμφυτον; ἔμφῠτος: "inborn, natural (...) implanted;" Liddell, p. 551.

224 Ὥστε ἀπορριζῶσαι μὲν τῆς σαρκὸς τὴν ἔμφυτον αὐτῆς ἐπιθυμίαν οὐκ ἔνεστι

as I said, it is possible through sobriety to prevent it from being emboldened against the mind,[225] especially in view of the fact that God's only-begotten Word was made man and no longer allows the law of sin to run riot in our members[226] (...) So we are not victorious[227] over nor completely uproot our implanted movements absolutely all at once; that is reserved for the life of total bliss we expect in the world to come.[228] But we are able to fight manfully and with God's help providing us with power from on high, we can rebuke[229] the movements of the flesh[230]."[231]

"This[232] must be understood to refer not to every kind of sin but only to capital crimes. In another place the aforesaid apostle declares that whoever does not

---

225 νήψει δὲ, ὡς ἔφην, οὐκ ἐάν καταθρασύνεσθαι τοῦ νοῦ, δυνατόν

226 μάλιστα ὅτι γέγονεν ἄνθρωπος ὁ μονογενής Λόγος τοῦ Θεοῦ, καὶ ἀγριανοντα τὸν νόμον τῆς ἁμαρτίας, τὸν ἐν τοῖς μέλεσιν ἡμῶν, οὐκ ἔτιν εανιεύεσθαι καθ' ἡμῶν συγκεχώρηκεν

227 Περιεσόμεθα; περιέχω: "overcome, gain the victory or advantage;" Liddell, p. 1373.

228 Περιεσόμεθα τοίνυν τῶν ἐμφύτων κινημάτων οὐκ εἰς ἄπαν, οὐδὲ ὁλοτελῶς (τοῦτο γὰρ τῇ παμμακαρίᾳ ζωῇ τετήρηται τῇ προσδοκωμένῃ ἔσεσθαι κατὰ τὸν αἰῶνα τὸν μέλλοντα)

229 ἐπιτιμῶσι; ἐπιτιμάω: "object to one as blameable (...) rebuke, censure, of persons;" Liddell, p. 667.

230 δυνάμεθα δὲ κατανδρίσασθαι, καὶ τοῖς τῆς σαρκὸς ἐπιπλήττειν κινήμασι, Θεοῦ συμπράττοντος, καὶ τὴν ἐξ ὕψους ἡμῖν χορηγοῦντος δύναμιν

231 Cyril of Alexandria. (1983). *Answers to Tiberius*. L. Wickham (Trans.), *Cyril of Alexandria: Select letters* (p. 171). Oxford: Oxford University Press.

232 1 Joh 3:9 & 5:18.

wish to avoid these or cleanse himself of them must not even be prayed for: 'Whoever knows that his brother is committing a sin that is not unto death, let him ask, and He will give life to those not sinning unto death. There is a sin unto death. I do not say that you should ask for it.'[233] But with regard to those which he declares are not unto death, from which even persons who faithfully serve Christ cannot be immune, however carefully they may conduct themselves, it is said: 'If we say that we have no sin, we deceive ourselves and there is no truth in us.'[234] And again: 'If we say that we have no sin, we make Him a liar and His word is not in us.'[235] For it is impossible for any of the holy ones not to fall into those small sins that are committed by word, by thought, by ignorance, by forgetfulness, by necessity, by will, and by surprise. Although these may be different than the sin which is said to be unto death, nonetheless they cannot be without guilt and blame."[236]

"We should protect our heart with such a sentinel of humility as to maintain the following understanding with a constant and unwavering intention: We can never attain to the dignity of such a purification (…) no one can be so circumspect in this world's struggle as not to be struck by at least the darts of infrequent and lesser sins, because it is impossible not to sin either through ignorance or carelessness or surprise or thought or

---

233 1 Jn 5:16.
234 1 Jn 1:8.
235 1 Jn 1:10.
236 Cassian, The Conferences, 416.

need or forgetfulness or in sleep. Even if someone has mounted to the splendid summit of virtue, so that he may pronounce the Apostle's words without boasting: 'For me it is a small matter that I be judged by you or by any human day. I do not even judge myself, for I am aware of nothing in myself,'[237] he should still realize that he cannot be without sin."[238]

"Whoever, then, ascribes sinlessness—that is, impeccability—to human nature must go against not empty words but the witness and proof of his own conscience, which is on our side, and he may declare that he is without sin only when he feels that he has not been snatched away from the highest good. For, indeed, whoever looks into his own conscience, to give but one example, and sees that he has attended even one synaxis without having been interrupted by any word or deed or thought may declare that he is sinless. So, since we confess that the flighty wandering of the human mind cannot be without all these idle and vain things, we must as a result truthfully confess that we cannot be without sin. For, with whatever carefulness a person may strive to keep watch over his own heart, he will never safeguard it according to the desire of his spirit, given the resistant character of the flesh. The more the human mind makes greater progress and attains to a more sincere purity of contemplation, the more unclean it will see itself in the mirror of its purity."[239]

---

237 1 Cor 4:3–4.
238 Cassian, The Conferences, 771.
239 Cassian, The Conferences, 811.

"Finally, if it is in our heart to investigate more carefully whether it is possible for a human being to possess sinlessness, from whom could we learn this more easily than from those who 'have crucified their flesh with its vices and lusts,'[240] and to whom the world has truly been crucified?[241] Although they have not only uprooted all of their vices but are even attempting to cut off the thought and the recollection of their sins, they nonetheless profess daily and faithfully that they cannot be free of the stain of sin for even a single hour."[242]

Some Words of Encouragement for when the Days Grow Dark and Cloudy[243]

"But by the bruised in heart, He means, those who have a weak and yielding mind, unable to resist the attacks of their passions, and so carried along by them, as to seem to be captives: to these He promises both healing and forgiveness[244]."[245]

"Be not troubled when you meditate upon the greatness of your former sins: but rather know, that

---

240 Gal 5:24.
241 Cf. Gal 6:14.
242 Cassian, The Conferences, 812–813.
243 Mar 4:35-38; don't worry…. By the Trinity's Grace they pass.
244 Συντετριμμένους δέ φησι τὴν καρδίαν, τοὺς ἀσθενεῖς καὶ εὐδιάθρυπτον ἔχοντας νοῦν, καὶ ταῖς τῶν παθῶν προσβολαῖς ἀντιφέρεσθαι μὴ δυναμένους, ὑπενηνεγμένους δὲ οὕτως αὐταῖς, ὡς αἰχμαλώτους εἶναι δοκεῖν. Τούτοις ἴασίν τε καὶ ἄφεσιν ἐπαγγέλεται
245 Cyril, Commentary on Luke, 61–62.

still greater is the grace that justifies the sinner, and absolves the wicked."[246]

"And this too we say; that though we are taught the falls of the saints in the sacred Scriptures, it is not that we may be caught in similar snares from disregarding the duty of steadfastness, but that if it do chance that we prove weak in anything that is necessary for salvation, we may not despair of being able once again to mount up unto fortitude, and, so to speak, recover our health after an unexpected illness."[247]

"And besides this, they ought not to forget that before Christ was seized, or Peter denied Him, he [Peter] had been a partaker of the Body of Christ, and of His precious Blood. 'For He took bread and blessed, and gave to them, saying, This is My Body. And in like manner also of the cup, saying, Drink of it all of you: for this is My Blood of the new covenant.'[248] Behold then, manifestly, that after having been a partaker of the mystical Eucharist, he fell into sin, and received forgiveness upon his repentance."[249]

"By telling them they should not be troubled, He placed them in the middle between hope and fear, so that for those who are weak and succumb to human frailty, the hope of mercy might help them to recover, while the fear of stumbling might urge them to fall

---

246 Cyril, Commentary on Luke, 161.

247 Cyril, Commentary on Luke, 700.

248 Mat 26:26.

249 Cyril, Commentary on Luke, 701.

only a few times. (They did not yet have the ability not to fall at all, since they were not yet clothed with power from above and from on high,[250] that is, the Grace that comes through the Spirit)."[251]

"Do not doubt, then, O man, nor think to yourself that if you approach Him repentantly, He will not grant you mercy readily. You have even now a pledge of what you hope for in prayer, which is hardly negligible; you already have a guarantee of His benevolence. Behold, He has flooded the whole land with river waters; behold how He still grants to sinners the enjoyment of the abundance of His customary provision. Your tears have not yet appeared, and God has continued to show Himself merciful. If He does not refuse to show pity to those who are not yet weeping, will He not rejoice in those who readily repent?"[252]

"A brother asked Abba Macarius, 'My father, I have committed a transgression.'[253] Abba Macarius said to him, 'It is written, my child, "I do not desire the death of a sinner so much as his repentance and his life."[254]

---

250 Lk 24:49.
251 Cyril, Commentary on John, Vol. 2, IVP Academic, 145.
252 Cyril of Alexandria. (2009). *Festal Letters, 1–12* (J. J. O'Keefe, Ed.; P. R. Amidon, Trans.; Vol. 118, p. 134). The Catholic University of America Press.
253 Literally: I have fallen into a transgression. "To fall" is an important concept in early monastic spirituality. Although the monk does not ask a question, the text uses *-shen* (*shini*), the verb ordinarily used for questions. "What do I do?" may be supplied.
254 Ezek 33:11; 1 Tim 2:4; 2 Pet 3:9.

Repent,[255] therefore, my child; you will see Him who is gentle, our Lord Jesus Christ, His face full of joy for you, like a nursing mother whose face is full of joy for her child. When he raises his hands and his face up to her, even if he is full of all kinds of uncleanness, she does not turn away from that bad smell and excrement[256] but takes pity on him and lifts him up and presses him to her breast, her face full of joy, and everything about him is sweet to her. If, then, this created person has pity for her child, how much greater is the love of the Creator, our Lord Jesus Christ, for us!'"[257]

Phase 2: Our Eternal Life After Our Resurrection

"Mankind then is perfected in Him and restored, as it was made at the beginning, in fact, with greater Grace.[258] For, on rising from the dead, we shall no longer fear death, but shall reign forever in Christ in the heavens."[259]

---

255 Both "repentance" (-*tastho*-) and "repent" (*kot*-) in Coptic convey the idea of (re)turning, turning back, as in Latin *convertere*.
256 *Nilahōj*. Crum, 150A, cites this passage and says the meaning is unknown; I have followed Am's translation, which Regnault and Guillaumont also follow.
257 Saint Macarius the Spiritbearer. (2004). *Saint Macarius the Spiritbearer: Coptic Texts Relating to Saint Macarius the Great* (J. Behr, Ed.; T. Vivian, Trans.; p. 104). St Vladimir's Seminary Press.
258 Τετελείωται οὖν ἐν αὐτῷ καὶ ἀποκατεστάθη ,ὥσπερ ἦν καὶ κατὰ τὴν ἀρχὴν γεγονός, τὸ ἀνθρώπινον γένος, καὶ μείζονι μᾶλλον χάριτι
259 Athanasius, Four Discourses against the Arians II.XXI.67, (NPNF² 4), 385.

"It is after that [the end of this age] that people will be kept at a distance—that is, after the Resurrection[260]—living a conspicuous and lengthy life, with the removal of all corruption, death done away with and all sin completely removed[261]."[262]

"For after the resurrection from the dead, there will be no longer the opportunity for love of the flesh, but the goad of sin will be entirely powerless.[263] That very (body) therefore which has been brought down to the earth, shall be clothed with incorruption[264]."[265]

Partaking or Participation is the Means by which We can, while in Phase 1, Begin to have God's Image and Likeness Restored within Us and Work with Him to Preserve It

"Therefore, in speaking of 'like' according to essence, we mean like from participation;[266] for 'likeness' is

---

260 μετὰ τὸν τῆς ἀναστάσεως

261 ἀνῃρημένης εἰς ἅπαν τῆς φθορᾶς, καὶ κατηργημένου τοῦ θανάτου, κα ἁπάσης ἁμαρτίας ἐξῃρημένης

262 Cyril of Alexandria. (2008). *Commentary on Isaiah* (R. C. Hill, Trans.; Vol. 1, p. 157). Holy Cross Orthodox Press.

263 Μετὰ γὰρ τὴν ἐκ νεκρῶν ἀνάστασιν, οὐκ ἔστιν ἔτι φιλοσαρκίας καιρός, ἀλλ' ἀπρακτήσει παντελῶς τῆς ἁμαρτίας τὸ κέντρον.

264 Αὐτὸ μέν τοι τὸ κατενεχθὲν εἰς τὴν γῆν, τὴν ἀφθαρσίαν ἐνδύσεται

265 Cyril, Commentary on Luke, 729.

266 Διὸ καὶ ὁ λέγων ὅμοιον κατ' οὐσίαν ἐκ μετουσίας τοῦ το λέγει ὅμοιον

a quality, which may attach[267] to essence,[268] and this would be proper to creatures, for they, by partaking, are made like God.[269] For 'when He shall appear,' says Scripture, 'we shall be like Him',[270] like, that is, not in essence but in sonship, which we shall partake from Him[271]."[272]

"And just as then it [humanity] was formed into the image of its Creator, so also now it is refashioned by participation in the Spirit to the likeness of its Maker[273]."[274]

"For God is the glorious and most beauteous Nature, while created things have a likeness with Him according to participation[275]."[276]

---

267 προσγένοιτ'; προσγίγνομαι: "attach oneself to another (...) to be added, accrue;" Liddell, p. 1505.
268 Τὸ γὰρ ὅμοιον ποιότης ἐστὶν, ἥτις τῇ οὐσίᾳ προσγένοιτ' ἄν
269 ταῦτα γὰρ ἐκ μετοχῆς ὁμοιοῦται τῷ Θεῷ
270 1 John 3:2.
271 ὅμοιοι δηλονότι οὐ τῇ οὐσίᾳ ἀλλὰ τῇ υἱότητι, ἧς μεταλαμβάνομεν παρ' αὐτοῦ
272 Athanasius, Councils of Ariminum and Seleucia 53, (NPNF² 4), 478–479.
273 Ωσπερ εμορφωθη τοτε κατ' εικονα του κτισαντος, ουτω και νυν τη του Πνευματος μετουσια προς εμφερειαν μεταπλαττεται του ιδιου ποιητου
274 Cyril, Commentary on John, Vol. 2, IVP Academic, 269-370.
275 Ἐν ὁμοιώσει δὲ τῇ πρὸς αὐτὸν κατὰ μέθεξιν, τὰ γενητά
276 Cyril of Alexandria. (2021). *On Veneration and Worship in Spirit and Truth: Book Nine*. (J. Gohl, Trans.; p. 26–27).

"A demonstration from holy Scripture that we are formed in the image of God by participation in Divinity[277]."[278]

We Partake of or Participate[279] in the Trinity

1. Passively

1. Through Divine Withdrawal of Grace

"Our virtue-loving God disciplines[280] us through suffering[281] and affliction[282].[283] For example, the prophet Isaiah says to us, 'The Lord will wash away the filth of the sons and daughters of Zion, and He will

---

277 Ἀπόδειξις ἀπὸ τῆς θείας Γραφῆς, ὅτιπερ ἐκ μετοχῆς τῆς πρὸς τὸ θεῖον κατ' εἰκόνα τὴν πρὸς αὐτὸ μορφούμεθα

278 Cyril of Alexandria. (2023). *Thesaurus of the Holy and Consubstantial Trinity.* (J. Tomes & M. Garcia, Trans.; p. 19). Greystone Theological Institute.

279 Some quotes do not expressly say we partake or participate; however, they should mention the recovery of some Divine Attribute, which could only occur through partaking or participation.

280 Παιδευει; παιδεύω: "bring up or rear (raise) a child (...) train and teach, educate (...) correct, discipline (...) chastise, punish;" Liddell, p. 1287.

281 Πονου; πόνος: "generally, toil, labour (...) of special kinds of labour, bodily exertion, exercise (...) stress, trouble, distress, suffering (...) also of disease (...) pain, esp. physical;" Liddell, p. 1448.

282 Θλιψεως; θλῖψις: "Pressure (...) oppression, affliction;" Liddell, p. 802.

283 Παιδευει γαρ ημας δια πονου και θλιψεως ο φιλαρετος ημων Θεος

purge out the blood from their midst with the Spirit of judgment and the Spirit of burning.'[284] Furthermore, the divinely inspired Paul says, 'If you endure discipline, God is treating you like children; for what child is there whom a father does not discipline?'[285]"[286]

Divine Withdraw *Can* be a Normal Unavoidable Part of a Healthy Spiritual Life:

"Amma Syncletica said, 'In the beginning there are a great many battles and a good deal of suffering for those who are advancing towards God and afterwards, ineffable joy. It is like those who wish to light a fire; at first they are choked by the smoke and cry, and by this means obtain what they seek (as it is said: "Our God is a consuming fire")[287]: so we also must kindle the divine fire in ourselves through tears and hard work.'"[288]

"An elder said, 'If the miller did not put the blindfold on the animal's eyes, it would turn about and eat the fruit of its labor. Similarly, by divine providence we received blindfolds so that we do not think highly of ourselves at the site of our good works and thus lose our reward. For this reason, from time to time we are left in unclean thoughts, and we only see them so

---

[284] Is 4:4.

[285] Heb 12:7.

[286] Cyril, Commentary on John, Vol. 2, IVP Academic, 218.

[287] Heb 12:24.

[288] *The Sayings of the Desert Fathers: The Alphabetical Collection,* Ward B., Trans.). (Kalamazoo: Cistercian Publications, 1975) Syncletica 1.

that we should condemn ourselves; and the unclean things themselves become a blindfold concealing the little good we do. For when a person blames himself, he does not lose his toil.'"[289]

"Abba Macarius said: 'The wiles of the Enemy are those called "night" and "darkness," as Paul said, "We do not belong to night, nor do we belong to darkness, but we belong to the day,"[290] for indeed the Son of God is the day and the Devil is the night. But if the heart passes by these wars, once again they besiege the combatant out of ill-will and then they begin to wage war on him with fornication and taking pleasure with children. On account of these wars, therefore, the heart is enfeebled so that it is impossible for the person to safeguard his purity as they make him aware of the seconds and minutes and the hardships of leading a life of virtue and how hard life is. As a result, great suffering and weariness come over the body. But if the heart grows weary in these matters and becomes enfeebled on account of the sufferings caused by these wars, if the person drives evil away from his heart and cries out to God, groaning in his soul and suffering, then the good God who has compassion for his creature sends a holy power that takes possession of the heart and gives him weeping and rejoicing and relief. As a result, he

---

[289] *The Book of the Elders: Sayings of the Desert Fathers - The Systematic Collection*, Wortley J., trans. (Collegeville: Liturgical Press, 2012), 15.100.
[290] 1 Th 5:5–8.

becomes stronger than the enmity opposing him[291] and his enemies are unable to prevail[292] against him because they are afraid of the power that has come upon him. As the apostle Paul proclaims, "Strive so that you may receive power."[293] For this is the power that Peter spoke about when he said, "There is an inheritance that is imperishable and incorruptible that is watching over you, who are being protected by the power of God through faith."[294] When the good God sees that the heart is strong against enmity, then he begins to withdraw the power from him. Seeing his free intention,[295] and making use of fear, [God] suddenly allows enmity into him in order to wage war against him with defilements and with the pleasure that comes from seeing and spiritual vanity and haughtiness. The person is like a rudderless ship drifting here and there. When the heart grows very weary on account of enmity, then God, who is good and has compassion for his creature, once again sends to him the holy power and it strengthens his soul and heart and body and all his other members beneath the yoke of the Paraclete, as our Savior Jesus Christ

---

291 Literally: "his enmity." The Coptic often changes Gk "enemy" to "enmity." See Antony Letter 1.24 (S. Rubenson, *The Letters of St. Antony: Monasticism and the Making of a Saint* [Minneapolis: Fortress, 1995], 198) where "enmity" is the primary reading with "the enemy" as a variant.

292 Both "prevail" and "strong" render Coptic *jemjom*, related to "power."

293 Acts 1:8 and Lk 13:24.

294 1 Pet 1:4.

295 Coptic *prohairesis* = Gk *proairesis*.

says: "Take my yoke upon you and learn from me, for I am gentle and humble of heart."[296] Then the good God begins to open "the eyes of the heart"[297] in order [for the person] to acknowledge and honor God with humility and contriteness of heart, as David says: "A sacrifice to God is a contrite and humble heart."[298] For from the sufferings caused by the wars, humility and contrition take root in the heart. Then the power reveals heavenly things to the mind and heart and [reveals] the songs and glory that will come to those who persevere, [and the power also reveals] that if the person endures numerous sufferings, these are insignificant compared with the honor that God will give to him, as the apostle once again says: "The sufferings of the present time are not worth comparing to the glory that will be revealed to us."[299] Then they begin to reveal the punishments before the heart and those who are being punished and many other things, all of which I am not able to declare. And the Paraclete establishes boundaries for the heart, that is, those things that make the soul and the other members pure,[300] and [establishes] great humility and watchfulness and an understanding of watchfulness, and the placing of oneself beneath all of creation, and [the ability] not to be concerned about the evil deeds of

---

296 Mt 11:29.
297 Eph 1:18.
298 Ps 50:19 (LXX). "Humble" (*tetapeinōmenēn*) is taken from the second part of v. 19, not quoted here.
299 Rom 8:18.
300 Literally: "the purities of the soul and the other members."

any person, and keeping the eyes pure,[301] and guarding the tongue,[302] and keeping the feet pure,[303] and working righteousness with the hands,[304] and worshiping with prayers, and mortification of the body, and the ability to keep vigil for God. These things are determined for him in moderation and with consideration, not to cause confusion but to bring about what is godly and proper. But if the understanding belittles the commandments of the Spirit, then the power withdraws and wars break out in the heart, and disturbances, and the passions of the body disturb him on account of the movements and attacks of the enemies. But if the heart turns about and keeps the commandments of the Spirit, it receives protection. Then the person knows that abiding with God is his rest, as David says: "Lord, because I have cried out to you, I have found the rest that I desired."[305] I am saying that unless a person possesses great humility in his heart and body, and debases himself in all things, and has a great ability to accept contempt, and suffers violence in all things, and keeps his death before him day after day, and renounces material things, and renounces the things of the flesh, he cannot keep the commandments of the Holy Spirit.'"[306]

---

301 34 Literally: "purity of the eyes."

302 Jas 3:5; 3:8.

303 Literally: "purity of the feet."

304 Literally: "justice/righteousness of the hands."

305 Ps 30:2.

306 Saint Macarius the Spiritbearer. (2004). *Saint Macarius the Spiritbearer: Coptic Texts Relating to Saint Macarius the Great* (Vivian T., Trans.; pp. 88–90). St. Vladimir's Seminary Press.

"After I had written my letter I remembered a certain word, and am moved to write to you about the trial of the soul of the man who is advanced, and who goes down to the depths of hell from the rank of spiritual perfection. It is of such a one that the Prophet cries, saying, 'You have delivered my soul from the depths of Hades.'[307] Trials will attach themselves to everyone who attaches himself to the Spirit of God, but as a result he acquires discernment and a different sort of splendor. Thus, when the prophet was going to be taken up, coming to the first heaven he wondered at its light; but when he came to the second he wondered so greatly as to say, 'I considered the light of the first to be darkness;'[308] and so on until the final stage of perfection. Therefore the soul of the perfectly righteous progresses and goes forward until it mounts to the heaven of heavens. If you attain this you have passed all trials. And there are even now men on earth who have reached this stage. I write to you, my beloved, so that you may firmly recognize that trials come upon the faithful not for their loss but for their advantage; and without trials being brought upon the soul it cannot mount to the place of Life, that is, of Him who created it. 'The Spirit breathes where it wills,'[309] and He breathes in souls that are pure and holy and righteous and good. And if they obey the Spirit, He gives them fear of God, and fervor, in the beginning. And when

---

307 Psa 86:13.
308 Ascension of Isaiah 8:21.
309 Joh 3:8.

He has sown His seed in them, it makes them hate all the world, be it gold or silver or ornaments, or father or mother or wife or children, and so it makes all the work of God sweeter to them than honey and the honey-comb, be it toil or fasting or vigil or stillness or works of mercy. And everything that is done for the sake of God thus becomes sweet for them, until He has taught them everything.[310] And when he has been taught all these things, a person is liable to be tried. And then all the things which before had seemed sweet to him weigh heavy upon him; that is why many, when they are tried, remain in heaviness and become carnal. These are they of whom it was said by Paul, 'Having begun in the Spirit, are you now being made perfect in the flesh? Have you suffered all these things in vain'[311] to no purpose? But if a man resists Satan in his first trial, and conquers him, then God gives him fervor which is peaceful, rational and persevering. For the first fervor is troubled and irrational. But the second fervor is better; and it gives birth to the capacity in a man to see spiritual things as he struggles in the great contest, having a patience that is unperturbed. For as with a ship when the wind is fair, her twin rudders are driven the more and so she travels a great distance, and so also the sailors rejoice and are at ease, so is the second fervor, bringing calm in every way. Now, my dear children, obtain for yourselves the second fervor, that you may be established in everything. For the

---

310 Jn 14:26.
311 Gal 3:1.

fervor which has God as its subject brings to nothing all the passions of flattery; it wipes away and blots out the oldness of the 'old man', and makes man to be a temple of God, as it is written, 'I will dwell in them and walk in them.'[312] If you desire that the fervor which is removed far from you should return again and come to you, this is the work that a man is required to do: he should make a covenant between himself and God, and cry out in passion of heart and say to Him, 'Forgive me for what I did in my neglectfulness; I will not continue in disobedience.' And then he should not walk anymore as under his own authority in order to satisfy his own will, either in body or soul, but rather his thoughts should be spread out before God, while he afflicts and rebukes his own soul, saying, 'How you have despised the good, and made light of your barrenness all these days!' You should remember all the torments, and the eternal kingdom, rebuking your soul at all times, saying to it, 'See what honor God gave you, and you have neglected and despised it.' When a man says this to his soul, rebuking it night and day, suddenly the fervor of God comes upon him, and this second fervor is greater than the first. For when blessed David saw the burden that had come upon him he said, 'I called to remembrance the eternal years and meditated thereon,'[313] and, 'I remembered the days of old, I meditated on all your works; I meditated on the works of your hands, and I stretched out my hands

---

312 2 Cor 6:17.
313 Psa 77:5.

unto you. My soul gasps for you as a thirsty land.'[314] And again Isaiah says, 'When you have turned back and moaned, then you will be saved, and will understand how it was with you.'[315]"[316]

2. Through Specific Salvific Works of God

i) The Incarnation

"For He has become Man, that He might deify us in Himself,[317] and He has been born of a woman, and begotten of a Virgin, in order to transfer to Himself our erring generation, and that we may become henceforth a holy race, and 'partakers of the Divine Nature,' as blessed Peter wrote[318]."[319]

"He came down into our estate and became a man, so that we ourselves 'might become partakers of His divine Nature,'[320] being joined to Him by partaking of the Holy Spirit and by the Grace of God[321]."[322]

---

314 Psa 143:5-6.

315 Isa 30:15 LXX.

316 *Letters of Ammonas*, Chitty D., trans. (Oxford: Sisters of the Love of God, 1979). Letter 10.

317 Γέγονε γὰρ ἄνθρωπος, ἵν'ἡμᾶς ἐν ἑαυτῷ θεοποιήσῃ

318 2 Pet. 1:4.

319 Athanasius, Personal Letters LX.4, (NPNF[2] 4), 576.

320 2 Pt 1:4.

321 τῇ τοῦ ἁγίου Πνεύματος μετοχῇ τε καὶ χάριτι Θεῷ συνδούμενοι

322 St. Cyril of Alexandria. (2018-2019). *Glaphyra on the Pentateuch: Genesis, Exodus through Deuteronomy* (N. P. Lunn, Trans.; Vol. 2, p. 94). The Catholic University of America Press.

ii) The Baptism and Anointing of Jesus Christ

"And if, as the Lord Himself has said, the Spirit is His, and takes of His, and He sends It,[323] it is not the Word, considered as the Word and Wisdom, who is anointed with the Spirit which He Himself gives,[324] but the flesh assumed[325] by Him which is anointed in Him and by Him[326]; that the sanctification coming to the Lord as man, may come to all men from Him.[327] For not of Itself, He says, does the Spirit speak, but the Word is He who gives It to the worthy[328]."[329]

---

323 αὐτοῦ ἐστι τὸ Πνεῦμα, ἐκ τοῦ αὐτοῦ λαμβάνει, αὐτός τε αὐτὸ ἀποστέλλει

324 αὐτοῦ διδομένῳ

325 προσληφθεῖσα

326 Elsewhere Athan. says that our Lord's Godhead was the immediate anointing or chrism of the manhood He assumed, *in Apollin.* ii. 3, *Orat.* iv. § 36. vid. Origen. *Periarch.* ii. 6. n. 4. And S. Greg. Naz. still more expressly, and from the same text as Athan. *Orat.* x. fin. Again, "This [the Godhead] is the anointing of the manhood, not sanctifying by an energy as the other Christs [anointed] but by a presence of Him whole who anointed, ὅλου τοῦ χρίοντος: whence it came to pass that what anointed was called man and what was anointed was made God." *Orat.* xxx. 20. *Damasc. F. O.* iii. 3. Dei Filius, sicut pluvia in vellus, toto divinitatis unguento nostram se fudit in carnem. *Chrysolog. Serm.* 60. It is more common, however, to consider that the anointing was the descent of the Spirit, as Athan. says at the beginning of this section, according to Luke 4:18; Acts 10:38.

327 ἵνα καὶ ὁ ἁγιασμὸς ,ὡς εἰς ἄνθρωπον τὸν Κύριον γινόμενος, εἰς πάντας ἀνθρώπους γένηται παρ' αὐτοῦ

328 ὁ Λόγος ἐστὶν, ὁ τοῦτο διδοὺς τοῖς ἀξίοις

329 Athanasius, Four Discourses against the Arians I.XII.47, (NPNF2 4), 334.

"The Spirit was in the prophets because of the need for prophesying. But now through Christ He dwells in believers, beginning in Him first when He became human. As God, there is no distance between Him and the Spirit, who springs from Him essentially and is His own Spirit.[330] But He is anointed for us and is said to receive the Spirit as a human being, acquiring participation in the divine Goods not for Himself but for human nature."[331]

iii) The Obedience and Submission of Jesus Christ

"Christ therefore has brought an end to the curse of the law for those who were subject to it, and had been unable to keep its enactments.[332] And in what way did He bring it to an end?[333] By fulfilling it.[334] And to put it in another way: in order that He might atone for the accusation of the transgression in Adam,[335] He showed Himself obedient and submissive in every respect to God the Father in our place."[336]

"What had succumbed had to—had to!—be healed and destroy death through the very flesh that was under the power of sin. When the flesh offended

---

330 Εχει μεν γαρ ως Θεος αδιαστατως το ουσιωδως εμπεφυκος αυτω, και ιδιον αυτου Πνευμα

331 Cyril, Commentary on John, Vol. 1, IVP Academic, 311-312.

332 Οὐκοῦν τῆς τοῦ νόμου κατάρας ἐξεπρίατο Χριστὸς τοὺς ὄντας μὲν ὑπὸ νόμον, οὐ μὴν ἔτι καὶ τετηρηκότας αὐτόν

333 Ἐξεπρίατο δὲ πῶς;

334 Πληρώσας αὐτόν

335 Ἵνα λύσῃ τῆς ἐν Ἀδὰμ παραβάσεως τὰ ἐγκλήματα

336 Cyril, Commentary on Luke, 19.

in Adam on account of his transgression, it fell under the power of death. In the same way when it became pleasing in Christ on account of His obedience, it was freed from the snares and fear of death."[337]

iv) The Proclamation of Jesus Christ as the Beloved Son of the Father

"In the same way He should be understood to receive the Father's love not for Himself (since He was always and forever loved), but He received this love from the Father when He became human in order to bestow the Father's love on us."[338]

v) The Sufferings and Crucifixion of Jesus Christ

"Why, when the Body was struck by the attendant, as suffering Himself He asked, 'Why do you hit Me[339]?' And being by nature intangible,[340] the Word yet said, 'I gave My back to the stripes, and My cheeks to blows, and hid not My face from shame and spitting[341].' For what the human Body of the Word suffered, this the Word, dwelling in the Body, ascribed to Himself, in order that we might be enabled to be partakers of the Godhead of the Word[342]."[343]

---

337 Cyril of Alexandria. (2022). *Commentaries on Romans, 1-2 Corinthians, and Hebrews* (J. C. Elowsky, G. L. Bray, M. Glerup, & T. C. Oden, Eds.; D. R. Maxwell, Trans.; p. 120). IVP Academic.

338 Cyril, Commentary on John, Vol. 2, IVP Academic, 307.

339 Jn 18:23.

340 ἄψαυστος

341 Isa 50:6.

342 τῆς τοῦ Λόγου θεότητος μετασχεῖν δυνηθῶμεν

343 Athanasius, Personal Letters LIX.6, (NPNF² 4), 572.

"For then again He went up to Jerusalem, and entered amid praises, and at that very time endured His saving passion in our behalf, that by suffering He might save, and renew unto incorruption the inhabitants of the earth."[344]

vi) The Death of Jesus Christ

"He endured it [death] not for Himself, but for the incorruptibility and salvation of all."[345]

"And when it happened that he fell from obedience into death and humanity fell from that original honor, God the Father re-created it and brought it back to newness of life through the Son, just as in the beginning. How did the Son bring it back? By the death of His holy Flesh He killed death and carried the human race back to incorruption.[346] After all, Christ was raised for us."[347]

vii) The Resurrection of Jesus Christ

"On the other hand, that as human beings had turned towards corruption He might turn them again to incorruptibility[348] and give them life from death, by making the body His own and by the grace of the resurrection banishing death from them."[349]

---

344 Cyril, Commentary on Luke, 470.
345 St. Athanasius the Great of Alexandria. (2011). *On the Incarnation: Translation* (J. Behr, Ed. & Trans.; p. 123). SVS Press.
346 Εις αναδρομην αφθαρσιας το ανθρωπινον γενος ανενεγκων
347 Cyril, Commentary on John, Vol. 2, IVP Academic, 369–370.
348 πάλιν εἰς τὴν ἀφθαρσίαν ἐπιστρέψῃ
349 St. Athanasius the Great of Alexandria. (2011). *On the Incarnation: Translation* (J. Behr, Ed. & Trans.; p. 67). SVS Press.

"For He arose from the dead, to be the way whereby not Himself so much but we rather return unto incorruption[350]."[351]

viii) The Ascension of Jesus Christ

"The Word, who in ancient times was devoid of humanity, now ascended as a human being to present Himself in a strange and unaccustomed way. This was for us and on our behalf so that, being found as a human being, He might hear along with all flesh in His power as the Son the words, 'Sit at my right hand.'[352] Thus He transferred the glory of adoption to the entire race through Himself (…) So He presented Himself as a human being on our behalf to the Father so that He might place us—we who departed from His presence because of the ancient transgression[353]—once again in the presence of the Father. He took His seat as Son so that we too might be called sons and children of God through Him (…) The dignity of His seat belongs to Christ by nature as the Son, and we can rightly and truly ascribe the glory of sitting there to Him and Him alone. But the fact that Christ who sits there is completely like us, in that He appeared as a man, while at the same time we understand Him to be God from God—that fact transfers, as it were, the Grace of that dignity also to us."[354]

---

350 ὁδὸς τῆς εἰς ἀφθαρσίαν ἀναδρομῆς, οὐχ ἑαυτῷ μᾶλλον, ἀλλ' ἡμῖν, γενόμενος

351 Cyril, Commentary on Luke, 724.

352 Ps 110:1 (Ps 109:1 lxx).

353 Δια την αρχαιαν παραβασιν

354 Cyril, Commentary on John, Vol. 2, IVP Academic, 148.

ix) The Giving of the Holy Spirit

"Therefore, they receive participation in the Holy Spirit when 'He breathed on them,' saying, 'Receive the Holy Spirit.'[355] After all, Christ could not have been lying. He would not have said 'receive' if He did not give."[356]

"And His own disciples He manifested partakers of the Holy Spirit, for He breathed on them,[357] saying, Receive the Holy Spirit[358]."[359]

2. Actively

1. Through Baptism

"All those after the Lord's coming have become—through baptism and the union with the Spirit—'sharers in[360] God's nature'[361] and are called sons of God."[362]

---

355 Οὐκοῦν δέχονται μὲν τὴν τοῦ ἁγίου Πνεύματος μέθηεξιν, ὅτε καὶ ἐνεφύσησεν αὐτοῖς, λέγων · ὁ Λάβετε Πνεῦμα ἅγιον

356 Cyril, Commentary on John, Vol. 2, IVP Academic, 370.

357 John 20:22.

358 Μετόχους δὲ τοῦ ἁγίου Πνεύματος τοὺς ἰδίους ἐνέφηνε [ἰσ.ἀνέφηνε] μαθητάς · ἐνεφύσησε γὰρ αὐτοῖς, λέγων · « Λάβετε Πνεῦμα ἅγιον»

359 Cyril of Alexandria. (1881). *Five Tomes against Nestorius; Scholia on the Incarnation; Christ Is One; Fragments against Diodore of Tarsus, Theodore of Mopsuestia, the Synousiasts* (p. 56). James Parker and Co.; Rivingtons.

360 This phrase does not mean that we become constituted or made up of the Divine Essence; rather, it is synonymous of the phrase "partaking of," and means that the Divine Essence shares grace or gifts with us.

361 2 Pet 1:4.

362 Cyril of Alexandria. Simonetti, M., ed. (2002). *Matthew 14-*

"You too must first be clothed with power from on high, must be made, that is, partaker of the Holy Spirit by means of precious baptism."[363]

"Therefore, Christ says that the one who is least in the kingdom of heaven, that is, the one who is already baptized, even though that person is not yet outstanding in works, is greater than John himself in this respect alone: while the blessed John was born of a woman, that person has been born of God, as it is written,[364] and has became a participant in the divine Nature,[365] having the Holy Spirit dwelling in them and now being called a temple of God."[366]

2. Through Chrismation

"It is when He [the Holy Spirit] is given by the Word that creatures participate in Him[367]."[368]

"When we receive the Spirit, we are made sons."[369]

---

28 (p. 109). InterVarsity Press.

363 Cyril, Commentary on Luke, 53.

364 1 Jn 3:9; cf. 1 Jn 5:18.

365 2 Pet 1:4.

366 Cyril, Commentary on John, Vol. 1, IVP Academic, 311.

367 παρ' οὗ διδόμενον μετέχεται παρὰ τῶν κτισμάτων

368 Athanasius and Didymus. (2011). *Works on the Spirit: Athanasius's Letters to Serapion on the Holy Spirit, and, Didymus's on the Holy Spirit* (J. Behr, Ed.; M. DelCogliano, A. Radde-Gallwitz, & L. Ayres, Trans.; Vol. 43, p. 95). St Vladimir's Seminary Press.

369 Ibid., 82.

3. Through Partaking of the True Body and Blood of Jesus Christ

"But finally the Bread from heaven, that is, Christ, nourishes us to eternal life both by supplying us with the Holy Spirit and by participation in His own Flesh, placing into us participation with God and destroying death that comes from the ancient Curse."[370]

"This is so that as they partake in the Blessing[371] that is from Him, they may now be made participants of the divine Nature and thus return[372] to incorruptibility and life and be remolded into the original form of our nature[373]."[374]

4. Through Repentance and Confession

"What in fact a son is, and of what is that name significant. In truth, Divine Scripture acquaints us with a double sense of this word (...) the first, which belongs to those who gain the Grace of the name from moral improvement, and receive power to become

---

370 Cyril, Commentary on John, Vol. 1, IVP Academic, 212.

371 The Eucharist.

372 Ανακομιζοιντο; ἀνακομίζω: "to be carried up-stream, or up the country (...) bring back, recover (...) bring or take back or away with one (...) Pass., to be brought back (...) and of persons, return, come or go back (...) bring back safe (...) restore to health, strengthen;" Liddell, p. 109.

373 Ινα της ευλογιας μετεσχηκοτες της απ' αυτου, κοινωμοι μεν ηδη της θειας αποτελοιντο φυσεως, ανακομιζοιντο δε ουτως εις αφθαρσιαν και ζωην, και εις το αρχαιον της φυσεως μεταπλαττοιντο σχημα

374 Cyril, Commentary on John, Vol. 1, IVP Academic, 214.

sons of God[375]."[376]

"For this is the work of the Father's loving-kindness and goodness, that not only should He make him alive from the dead, but that He should render His Grace illustrious through the Spirit. Therefore, instead of corruption, He clothes him with an incorruptible garment; instead of hunger, He kills the fatted calf; instead of far journeys, [the Father] watched for his return, providing shoes for his feet; and, what is most wonderful, placed a divine signet-ring upon his hand; whilst by all these things He begat him afresh in the image of the glory of Christ. These are the gracious Gifts of the Father, by which the Lord honors and nourishes those who abide with Him, and also those who return to Him and repent."[377]

"By striving with all our might to do whatever is good and by setting our mind above the pleasures of the flesh, we may preserve intact the beauty of the image that is implanted in us.[378] This is the spiritual life, and this is the meaning of worship in the Spirit[379]."[380]

---

375 Εἰ μὲν οὖν κατὰ τὴν πρώτην, οἷοί εἰσι καὶ οἱ ἐκ βελτιώσεως τρόπων ἐπικτώμενοι τὴν τοῦ ὀνόματος χάριν, καὶ λαμβάνοντες ἐξουσίαν, ἵνα υἱοὶ Θεοῦ γένωνται

376 Athanasius, De Decretis or Defence of the Nicene Definition III.6, (NPNF² 4), 154.

377 Athanasius, Festal Letters VII.10, (NPNF² 4), 527.

378 Εφεσει τη προς παν οτιουν αγαθον ολοσχερως ανακειμενοι, και φιλασαρκιας κρειττονα την διανοιαν εχοντες, απαραποιητον εν εαυτοις της εντεθεισης εικονος το καλλος τηρησωμεν

379 Ουτος γαρ ο Βιος ο πνευματικος, αυτή της εν Πνευματι λατρειας η δυναμις

380 Cyril, Commentary on John, Vol. 2, IVP Academic, 297.

There are a myriad of activities, both mental and physical, that fall under this category; some notable examples include:

i) Acts of Love

"The wise John himself will show us how we are in Christ and He in us when he says, 'By this we know that we are in Him and He is in us: by the Spirit whom He has given us.'[381] And again, 'By this we know that we are in Him: whoever claims to abide in Him ought to walk just as He walked.'[382] And he makes this even clearer to his hearers by saying, 'Whoever keeps His commandments abides in Him and He in them.'[383] Now if keeping the commandments works love toward Him, and we are united to Him through love,[384] how could his statement in this passage not be clearly true?"[385]

Practical Ways to Show Love: "Not only does he take pains to teach that one must value love for God and for one another; he also shows how one may be seen to practice it. He goes on as follows: 'Love is patient, love is kind, love is not jealous or boastful; it is not arrogant or rude. It does not seek its own interests; it is not irritable or resentful; it does not rejoice at wrong, but rejoices in the right; it bears all things, believes all

---

381 1 Jn 3:24.
382 1 Jn 2:5–6.
383 1 Jn 3:24.
384 Κολλωμεθα δε δια της αγαπης αυτω
385 Cyril, Commentary on John, Vol. 2, IVP Academic, 211.

things, hopes all things, endures all things. Love never ends'[386]."[387]

ii) Contemplating the Holy Trinity

"But because of his likeness to the One who Is,[388] which, if he had guarded through his consideration[389] (thinking deeply about) of Him,[390] his natural corruption would have lost its force[391],[392] he would have remained[393] incorruptible,[394] just as Wisdom says, 'Attention to the laws is the confirmation of incorruptibility.'[395] And being incorruptible, he would have lived thereafter like God[396]."[397]

---

386 1 Cor 13:4-8.
387 Cyril of Alexandria. (2009). *Festal Letters, 1-12* (J. J. O'Keefe, Ed.; P. R. Amidon, Trans.; Vol. 118, p. 129). The Catholic University of America Press.
388 Διὰ δὲ τὴν πρὸς τὸν ὄντα ὁμοιότητα
389 Κατανοήσεως; κατανοησις: "observation, consideration;" Liddell, p. 902.
390 ἣν εἰ ἐφύλαττε διὰ τῆς πρὸς αὐτὸν κατανοήσεως
391 ἤμβλυνεν; ἀμβλύνω: "Metaphorically (...) lose its edge or force;" Liddell, p. 78.
392 ἤμβλυνεν ἂν τὴν κατὰ φύσιν φθοράν
393 ἔμεινεν; μένω: "of things, to be lasting, remain, stand (...) of condition, remain as one was;" Liddell, p. 1103.
394 ἔμεινεν ἄφθαρτος
395 Wis 6:18.
396 ἄφθαρτος δὲ ὤν, ἔζη λοιπὸν ὡς Θεός
397 St. Athanasius the Great of Alexandria. (2011). *On the Incarnation: Translation* (J. Behr, Ed. & Trans.; p. 59). SVS Press.

iii) Prayer

"Ask therefore the bestowal without limitation of spiritual gifts. Ask strength, that you may be able manfully to resist every fleshly lust. Ask of God an uncovetous disposition; long suffering; gentleness; and the mother and nurse of all good, I mean, patience. Ask calmness of temper; self-control; a pure heart; and further, ask also the wisdom that comes from Him. These things He will give readily: these save the soul: these work in it that better beauty, and imprint in it God's image."[398]

5. These Opportunities are Why the Life of the Church is Sometimes Called the Mystical or Sacramental Life

"Now, it should be understood that the reality of the promise comes also in the form of sacramental[399] fulfillment; the living water of holy baptism[400] is given to us as *rain*, the Bread of Life[401] as *grain*, and the Blood[402] as *wine*. Use of oil is also applied in bringing those justified in Christ to maturity through holy Baptism."[403]

Mystical: The Greek root being the verb μυέω: "to be initiated in a thing."[404] Hence the Mysteries of

---

398 Cyril, Commentary on Luke, 361.
399 μυστικῆς
400 ἁγίου βαπτίσματος
401 ὁ ἄρτος τῆς ζωῆς
402 τὸ αἷμα
403 Cyril of Alexandria. (2007). *Commentary on the Twelve Prophets* (T. P. Halton, Ed.; R. C. Hill, Trans.; Vol. 115, p. 292). The Catholic University of America Press.
404 Liddell, p. 1150.

the Church initiate the process of the restoration of God's image and likeness within us.

Sacramental: Sacrament is an old French word, coming from the Latin word "sacramentum," which comes from the Latin verb "sacrare," which means "to make holy." Hence the Sacraments of the Church initiate the process of the restoration of God's image and likeness within us, specifically the Divine Attribute of holiness.

Summary of the Spiritual Life

The spiritual life, which is the restoration and preservation of God's image and likeness within us, *is* salvation. We are to continually work towards the goal of preserving the image of God that has been implanted in us. Being in God's image and likeness means to possess *some* Divine Attributes. The Holy Trinity shares *some* of Its Divine Attributes with humans; the process of an object receiving attributes is called partaking or participation. There are active and passive ways by which we can partake of the Holy Trinity. Some active ways are only performed once in a person's life, namely baptism and chrismation, whereas others are to be done continually throughout a person's life, specifically partaking of Christ's Body and Blood, repentance, and confession. For the *entirety* of our earthly lives, we are to *frequently* partake of the true Body and Blood of Jesus Christ, *relentlessly* pursue and live a life of repentance and patiently accept and endure, with a *thankful* and *joyful* heart, whatever the Holy Trinity does in our lives.

"Spirituality" is Related to the Spiritual Life and Means the Characteristic of Being Spiritual

"Spiritual" means living according to the guidance of the Holy Spirit.

"And though you hear the sacred Scripture say of the human body, that 'it is sown a natural[405] body, it is raised a spiritual body,'[406] do not deny the return even of human bodies to incorruption.[407] For as the 'natural' is that which follows after, and is subject to nature, that is, to fleshly lusts, so also the 'spiritual' is that which submits itself to the will of the Holy Spirit."[408]

"Being spiritual means that one does not live according to the flesh but rather inclines away from it and toward the will to follow what the Spirit wants[409]."[410]

---

405 ψυχικός: "the natural man, opposed to ὁ πνευματικός (the spiritual);" Liddell, p. 2028.
406 1 Cor 15:44.
407 μὴ ἀνέλῃς τῶν ἀνθρωπίνων σωμάτων τὴν εἰς ἀφθαρσίαν ἀναδρομήν
408 Cyril, Commentary on Luke, 729.
409 Νοεῖται δὲ πνευματικὸς ὁ μὴ κατὰ σάρκα ζῶν, ἀπνενευκὼς δὲ μᾶλλον ἐπὶ τὸ θέλειν ἕπεσθαι τῇ θελήσει τοῦ πνεύματος
410 Cyril of Alexandria. (2022). *Commentaries on Romans, 1-2 Corinthians, and Hebrews* (J. C. Elowsky, G. L. Bray, M. Glerup, &

As was mentioned above, God wants His image and likeness within us to be restored, which was also shown to be the goal of the spiritual life; thus, pursuing the goal of the spiritual life is synonymous with being spiritual.

Further, since this same description of being spiritual is also mentioned by St. Paul,[411] it is evident that this understanding is the correct and true idea or opinion, which is the meaning of the word ortho[412]-dox,[413] on what it means to be spiritual.

Therefore, the spirituality mentioned above can also correctly be called orthodox spirituality; thus, the spiritual life is synonymous with orthodox spirituality.

T. C. Oden, Eds.; D. R. Maxwell, Trans.; p. 14). IVP Academic.

411 Rom 8:14.

412 Ορθος: "right, true, correct (...) real, genuine;" Liddell, H. G. (1996). A lexicon: Abridged from Liddell and Scott's Greek-English lexicon (p. 567). Oak Harbor, WA: Logos Research Systems, Inc.

413 Δόξᾰ: "a notion (...) an opinion, judgment;" Liddell, H. G. (1996). A lexicon: Abridged from Liddell and Scott's Greek-English lexicon (p. 209). Oak Harbor, WA: Logos Research Systems, Inc.

Principles of the Spiritual Life

1. A Balance Between Labors and Sinless Leisure Time[414] is *Necessary* in the Spiritual Life

"A hunter in the desert saw Abba Anthony enjoying himself with the brethren and he was shocked. Wanting to show him that it was necessary sometimes to meet the needs of the brethren, the old man said to him, 'Put an arrow in your bow and shoot it.' So he did. The old man then said, 'Shoot another,' and he did so. Then the old man said, 'Shoot yet again,' and the hunter replied 'If I bend my bow so much I will break it.' Then the old man said to him, 'It is the same with the work of God. If we stretch the brethren beyond measure they will soon break. Sometimes it is necessary to come down to meet their needs.' When he heard these words the hunter was pierced by compunction and, greatly edified by the old man, he went away. As for the brethren, they went home strengthened."[415]

"Although the pleasant interval of relaxation and hospitality, which usually occurs upon the arrival of the brothers, may seem annoying and worth avoiding

---

414 See Mar 6:31; ἀναπαύσασθε; ἀναπαύω: "make to cease, stop or hinder from a thing (...) rest, make to halt (...) bring to a close (...) take rest (...) take rest from (...) halt, rest (...) to be relieved from (...) regain strength;" Liddell, p. 115.

415 Ward, Benedicta. *The Sayings of the Desert Fathers – The Alphabetical Collection*; (Kalamazoo: Cistercian Publications, 1975), 3.

to you, nonetheless listen patiently for a while to how beneficial and salutary[416] it is for both our body and our spirit. It often happens even to the most experienced and to the perfect, to say nothing of novices and the weak, that, unless the intensity and the severity of their mind have been softened by some break for the sake of change, they fall into lukewarmness of spirit or at least into serious bodily ill health. Therefore, when even frequent visits from the brothers interrupt them, the prudent and the perfect should not only bear them patiently but even embrace them gratefully. First, they move us to desire ever more passionately the recesses of the desert, because, although they are somehow believed to impede our progress, they keep it unwearied and constant. If a person were not occasionally slowed down by some obstacle he would not be able to hold out until the end with untiring swiftness. Then, they indulge with the fruit of hospitality the feeble body's need for refreshment, conferring on us greater gain with this very pleasant break than what it would have acquired by the fatigue of abstinence. In this regard I shall briefly recount a very appropriate story that has been circulating for a long time. It is said that the most blessed John, when he was softly petting a bird[417] with his hands, suddenly saw a certain philosopher approaching him dressed like a hunter. He [the philosopher] marveled that a man of such a respectable reputation would

---

416 Promoting good health and wellbeing.
417 Specifically a partridge.

submit himself to pleasures so small and lowly. 'Are you not,' he said, 'the John whose extraordinary and celebrated reputation drew me to you as well with the greatest desire to make your acquaintance? Why, then, are you occupied with such contemptible pleasures?' The blessed John said: 'What are you carrying in your hand?' And he said: 'A bow.' 'And why,' he asked, 'do you not always carry it about everywhere pulled tight?' He replied to him: 'That is not supposed to be done. Constant bending would lessen its tensile strength, and it would be weakened and ruined. Then, once the tension had been lost by excessive and continual bending, when I had to shoot heavier arrows at some animal, a stronger blow could not be struck.' 'Nor,' said the blessed John, 'should this small and brief recreation of our mind offend you, young man. If by a certain relaxation it did not occasionally lighten and loosen its tight tension, it would not be able to listen to the power of the spirit when necessity demanded, since it would be weakened by its unrelenting exertion.'"[418]

2. Balance or Moderation is to Regulate Even the Spiritual Things We do

"Nor can another reason be found for their fall, except that they were less well instructed by the elders and were utterly unable to grasp the meaning of discretion, which avoids excess of any kind and

---

418 Cassian, The Conferences, 841-842.

teaches the monk always to proceed along the royal road and does not let him be inflated by virtues on the right hand—that is, in an excess of fervor to exceed the measure of a justifiable moderation by a foolish presumption—nor let him wander off to the vices on the left hand because of a weakness for pleasure—that is, under the pretext of controlling the body [from performing excessive asceticism], to grow soft because of a contrary lukewarmness of spirit."[419]

"If we weigh and examine everything that we do with a reasonable mind and always, out of the purity of our heart, take into consideration not others' judgments but our own conscience, it is certain that this interval of relaxation will be unable to damage a just strictness. But this will only be so if, as has been said, an unsullied mind weighs the proper measure of indulgence and abstinence on an accurate scale and chastises equally an excess on either side, distinguishing with true discretion whether the weight of pleasure is pressing down our spirit or a more strict abstinence is tipping it to the other side, that of the body, and either lowering or raising the part that it thinks is too light or too heavy. For our Lord wants nothing to be done for His worship and honor without the moderating force of judgment."[420]

---

419 Cassian, The Conferences, 84-85.
420 Cassian, The Conferences, 735.

Discernment is Needed to Safely Navigate One's Spiritual Life

"What was discussed at great length was what virtue or observance could keep a monk permanently unharmed by the snares and deceptions of the devil and bring him up on the right path and with sure steps to the summit of perfection (…) And when they had thus determined that more certain access to God could be obtained by different virtues and the greater part of the night had been taken up with this question, blessed Antony finally spoke: 'All the things that you have mentioned are indeed necessary and useful for those who thirst for God and who desire to come to him. But the innumerable falls and experiences of many people do not at all permit us to attribute the highest grace to these things (…) Therefore we would be able to know clearly what was the best way to come to God if we carefully sought out the reason for the ruin and deception of these people. For although the works of the aforesaid virtues abounded in them, the lack of discretion by itself did not permit those works to endure to the end.'"[421]

"Surely none of these men would have been so tragically deluded if they had made an effort to follow the rule of discretion. Thus the falls and experiences of many show how dangerous it is not to have the grace of discretion."[422]

---

421 Ibid., 84–85.
422 Ibid., 90–91.

One Should Build a Spiritual Life around One's Abilities

"It behooves each one of us to gauge the measure of his strength carefully beforehand and to follow the discipline that is in keeping with his abilities because, although all things are beneficial, nonetheless not all things can be fitting for all people. Although the anchorite life is good, we see that it is not appropriate for everyone."[423]

3. Orthodox Spirituality *Requires* Conscious Purpose of Mind

Abba Anthony said, "Whoever hammers a lump of iron, first decides what he is going to make of it, a scythe, a sword, or an axe. Even so we ought to make up our minds what kind of virtue we want to forge or we labor in vain."[424]

"Do not think or do anything without having a purpose directed to God; the person who journeys without direction will have labored in vain."[425]

"Hence, too, the end of our course is the kingdom of God. But we should inquire carefully into the nature of our goal. If we have not in similar fashion grasped this we

---

[423] Ibid., 830–831.

[424] Ward, Benedicta. *The Sayings of the Desert Fathers – The Alphabetical Collection.* (Kalamazoo: Cistercian Publications, 1975), 8.

[425] Mark the Monk. (2009). Counsels on the Spiritual Life (J. Behr, Ed.; T. Vivian & A. Casiday, Trans.; Vols. 1 & 2, p. 97). St Vladimir's Seminary Press.

shall be wearied fruitlessly by our toil, because if the road is uncharted, then those who undertake the hardships of the journey will have nothing to show for it."[426]

There are plenty of starving people, made to unwillingly fast, that do not have a deep relationship with the Holy Trinity; performing a godly external action will not help us in our relationship with the Holy Trinity if we do not also have a godly purpose in our soul as the root of the action.

This is why being content with external labors and not being concerned about one's internal motives is a pernicious danger of the spiritual life.

4. Pursuing the Restoration of God's Image and Likeness within Us, or Purity of Heart, is to be the Motive Behind all of Our Actions

"For it is for its sake [cultivating purity of heart] that we do and endure everything (…) so that perpetual purity of heart may be kept."[427]

"These observances [ascetic exercises and labors] do not exist for themselves. If perchance we are unable to carry out some strict obligation of ours because we are prevented by some good and necessary business, we should not fall into sadness or anger or indignation, which we would have intended to drive out by doing what we omitted. For what is gained by fasting is

---

426 Cassian, The Conferences, 43.
427 Ibid., 44.

less than what is spent on anger, and the fruit that is obtained from reading is not so great as the loss that is incurred by contempt for one's brother. It behooves us, then, to carry out the things that are secondary—namely, fasts, vigils, the solitary life, and meditation on Scripture—for the sake of the principal scopos,[428] which is purity of heart or love, rather than for their sake to neglect this principal virtue which, as long as it remains integral and intact, will prevent anything bad from happening to us whenever one of the things that are secondary has to be omitted out of necessity. For it will be of no use to have fulfilled everything if this primary object, for the sake of attaining which all things are to be pursued, has been lost."[429]

Anything that can Facilitate This Should be Welcomed

"Whatever therefore can direct us to this scopos [immediate goal],[430] which is purity of heart, is to be pursued with all our strength, but whatever deters us from this is to be avoided as dangerous and harmful."[431]

This is the case even if the thing is undesirable: "For everything, however beneficial and necessary it may appear, should nonetheless be put aside in order to avoid the disturbance of anger, and everything that may seem

---

[428] Σκοπός: "mark or object on which one fixes the eye (...) aim, end, object;" Liddell, p. 1614.
[429] Cassian, The Conferences, 45–46.
[430] Σκοπός: "mark or object on which one fixes the eye (...) aim, end, object;" Liddell, p. 1614.
[431] Cassian, The Conferences, 44.

unfriendly should be put up with and tolerated in order to maintain unharmed the tranquility of love and peace."[432]

Anything that can Harm This Should be Rejected

"Whatever may disturb the purity and tranquility of our mind, then, however useful and necessary it may appear, must be avoided as harmful."[433]

This is the case even if something seems beneficial or necessary: "He will esteem nothing more of a loss than anger and nothing more precious than a peaceful mind and a heart that is always pure. On their account are to be spurned the advantages not only of carnal things but even of those that seem to be spiritual, if they cannot be acquired and perfected other than by disturbing this tranquility."[434]

Sometimes Ascetic and Spiritual Exercises can Cause Harm if not Abstained from

"And, to mention nothing else, there are many who exalt themselves above their neighbors, thereby causing great mischief. For the boast of fasting did no good to the Pharisee, although he fasted twice a week, only because he exalted himself against the publican. In the same manner the Word blamed the children of Israel on account of such a fast as this, exhorting them by Isaiah the Prophet, and saying, 'I did not choose this

---

432 Ibid., 562.

433 Ibid., 46.

434 Ibid., 681.

fast, and such a day for a man to humble his soul; not even if you should bow down your neck like a hook, and should spread sackcloth and ashes under you; neither thus shall you call the fast acceptable'[435]."[436]

"The essentially best thing, then, is that on account of which the indifferent things are done. This chief good itself, however, is not pursued for any reason other than its own goodness alone. This is distinguished from others, which we have spoken of as indifferent, in these ways: if it is good by itself and not by reason of something else; if it is necessary for its own sake and not for the sake of something else; if it is unchangeably and always good, constantly retaining its own character and never being able to become its opposite; if its removal or cessation cannot but bring on the gravest evil; if, similarly, the essential evil, which is its opposite, cannot ever become good. These defining elements, by which the character of the essential goods is distinguished, can never be applied to fasting. For it is neither good by itself nor necessary for its own sake, because it is properly exercised for the sake of acquiring purity of heart and body, so that the stings of the flesh might be dulled and a peaceful mind reconciled to its Creator. Nor is it unchangeably and always good, because we are not ordinarily hurt by its absence; indeed, sometimes when it is done inopportunely it ruins the soul. Nor is that which seems opposed to it—that is, the naturally enjoyable taking of food—an essential evil."[437]

---

435 Is 58:5.

436 Athanasius, Festal Letters I.4, (NPNF2 4), 507–508.

437 Cassian, The Conferences, 732.

Ascetic and Spiritual Exercises do not have Any Value of Themselves, but Derive Their Value from the Ability to Cultivate Purity of Heart

"Therefore, since every virtue is summed up and fulfilled in the form and habit of love, let us not think highly of ourselves for fasting or sleeping on the ground or other burdens of asceticism if we do not carefully preserve love for the brother. Otherwise, we will be carried wide of the turning posts like unskilled charioteers, and we will wander off course like a pilot who holds the ship's rudder but who ignorantly misses the destination of the voyage (…) I think that to boast in physical labors while falling short of the more important and necessary virtues is to fail at progressing toward the goal."[438]

"For mercy, patience, and love, as well as the precepts of the aforementioned virtues, in which the good is an essential one, are not to be exercised on account of fasting, but rather fasting on account of them. An effort must be made to acquire by fasting those virtues which are truly good, and not to turn the exercise of the virtues toward the goal of fasting. The affliction of the flesh is beneficial and the medicine of hunger should be taken in order that thereby we might be able to attain to love. Therein lies the permanent good, which is stable and not subject to the vicissitudes of time."[439]

---

438 Cyril, Commentary on John, Vol. 2, IVP Academic, 141.
439 Cassian, The Conferences, 731–732.

5. There are Varying Degrees within the Spiritual Life

"For He desired, as He testified in Ezekiel,[440] the repentance of a man rather than his death; so that evil should be entirely consumed in all men, that the soul, being purified, might be able to bring forth fruit; for the word which is sown by Him will be productive, some thirty, some sixty, some an hundred[441]."[442]

"The God of all, after all, being righteous and no respecter of persons, accepts people rather according to the measure of spiritual maturity, whether parents, or still children, adolescents or young adults in a spiritual sense."[443]

"Although these three [fear of punishment, hope for rewards, and love of God] seem to tend to one end, inasmuch as they move us to abstain from what is unlawful, nonetheless they differ from one another by considerable degrees of excellence. For the first two belong properly to those who are tending toward perfection and have not yet acquired a love of virtue, but the third belongs particularly to God and to those who have received in themselves the image and likeness of God. For only he does what is good who is moved not by fear or by the hope of reward but by a disposition for the good alone."[444]

---

440 Ezek. 18:23, 32.
441 Mark 4:20.
442 Athanasius, Festal Letters III.4, (NPNF² 4), 514.
443 Cyril of Alexandria. (2008). *Commentary on Isaiah* (R. C. Hill, Trans.; Vol. 2, p. 93). Holy Cross Orthodox Press.
444 Cassian, The Conferences, 412.

6. Sometimes One will be Called Away from a Good Pursuit and the Intensity to Pursue It by God for a Good Reason

"The Apostle says: 'We wanted to come to you time and again, but Satan hindered us.'[445] Thus we sometimes feel ourselves called away for a good reason even from spiritual concerns, so that, as the intensity of our pursuit is unwillingly interrupted and we give in somewhat to the weakness of our flesh, we may learn—even against our will—a salutary patience. The blessed Apostle says something similar about this plan of God: 'Therefore I asked the Lord three times that this would leave me. And he said to me: My grace is sufficient for you, for strength is perfected in weakness'[446]."[447]

Glory be to the Incomprehensible Holy Trinity: The Father, Son and Holy Spirit; one God, indivisible and uncompounded in His Essence, manifold in His Attributes. Amen.

---

445 1 Thes 2:18.

446 2 Cor 12:8–9.

447 Cassian, The Conferences, 471.

Illustrations

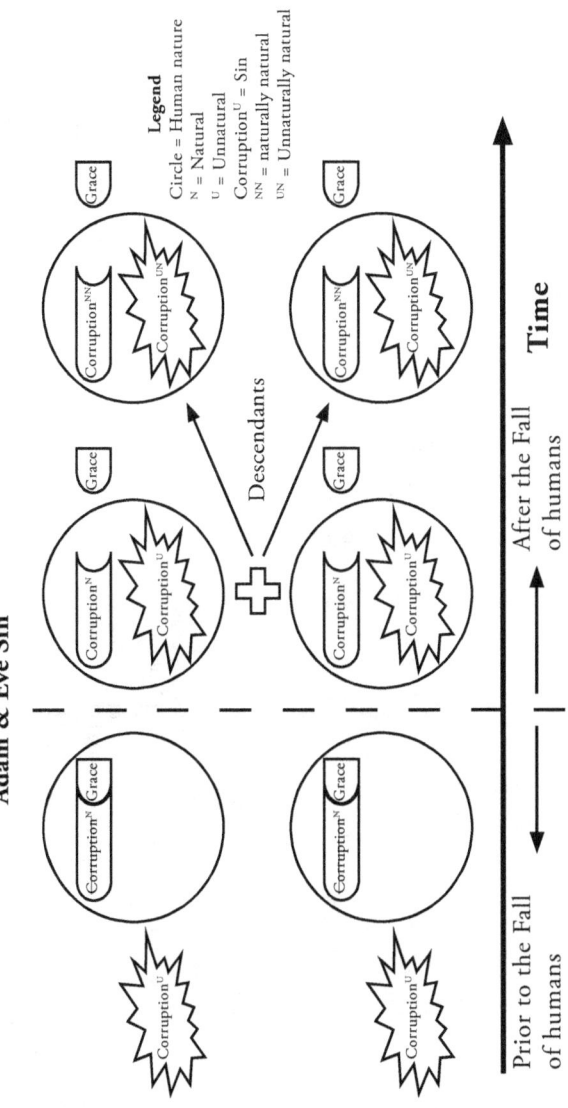

2. The Process of Salvation (Partaking) According to Orthodox Christianity

Prior to Time, the Holy Trinity alone existed — The Holy Trinity

United to the Holy Trinity — The Holy Trinity / Humans

1) After creating time, the Holy Trinity created humans; His only motivation for this was love.
2) Since the Holy Trinity loves us He created us united to the most enjoyable Thing, Himself.
3) Being united to the Holy Trinity allows humans to partake of, and thus receive **certain** Attributes from, the Holy Trinity; notably:
   i. Goodness
   ii. Incorruptibility
   iii. Immortality
4) Synonyms for receiving **some** of the Holy Trinity's Attributes, and thus existing in a supernatural state, include:
   i. Being made in God's Image and Likeness
   ii. Deification (Theopoiesis)
   iii. Participating in the Divine Nature

Separated from the Holy Trinity — The Holy Trinity / Humans

1) Humans, through sin, which is inappropriately using free will and setting it contrary to the Holy Trinity, destroyed their union with Him.
2) Loss of union with the Holy Trinity causes us to no longer partake of Him; thus, we lose the aforementioned Attributes, and become subject to their opposites:
   i. Evil
   ii. Decay
   iii. Death
3) Because humans cannot escape death, or come back from it on their own, it is clear that the effects of our disrupted union with the Holy Trinity are:
   i. Beyond our abilities to reverse
   ii. Permanent

Reunited to the Holy Trinity — The Holy Trinity / Humans

1) Salvation, which is being reunited to, partaking of and receiving Attributes of the Holy Trinity which were lost, is the result of the Holy Trinity and humans working **together**.
2) The Holy Trinity, because He loves us, initiates our salvation and brings us towards it through:
   A. Divine withdrawal (removal of Grace)
   B. Salvific works, such as:
      i. The Incarnation of the Son of God
      ii. The Baptism/Chrismation of Jesus Christ
      iii. The suffering, Crucifixion and death of Jesus Christ
      iv. The Resurrection of Jesus Christ
      v. The Ascension of Jesus Christ
      vi. Jesus Christ giving the Gift of the Holy Spirit
3) Humans, in order to benefit from these, must respond and conform to His Divine Will; this is accomplished through living the Sacramental Life
4) We receive a pledge of our being reunited to the Holy Trinity in this life, and it is fulfilled in its entirety in the eternal life.

Time

3. Insight into Divine Withdrawal

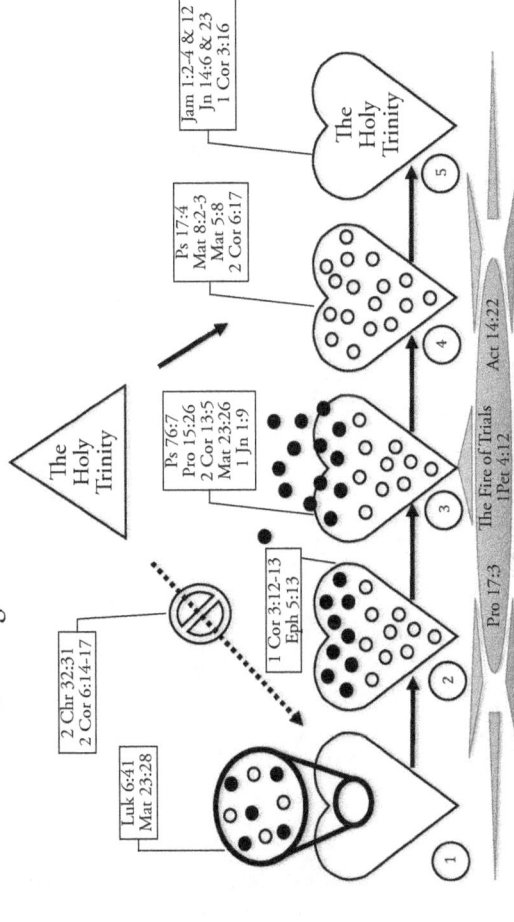

Insight into Divine withdrawal (Abandonment by God/Removal of Grace):
1) The Holy Trinity will withdraw from a person to help that person become aware of his/her sins—secret sins (Ps 18:13 LXX).
2) Trials and temptations can allow opportunity for one's faults to come to the surface, become visible and be identified.
3) Empowered with the knowledge of one's weaknesses, one can now bring these to the Trinity to be healed of them.
4) Having gone to the Trinity asking for healing in a spirit of humility, one will receive healing, and then begin seeing the Trinity dwell within oneself more.
5) Patiently enduring this process of trials and healing, one is brought to perfection and will have the crown of life and deep intimacy with the Trinity.

4. Humans were Created Initially Existing in the Image and Likeness of God

1) "The Word of the Father after Whose likeness they [humans] were originally made. For the soul is made after the image and likeness of God."[1]

2) "So our forefather Adam was made, according to the faith contained in the sacred Scriptures, in the image and likeness of God."[2]

Being in God's Image and Likeness Means Receiving Some Divine Attributes

1) "For you know yourselves, and no one can dispute it, that 'like' is not based on essence, but on properties, and qualities; for in the case of essences we speak, not of likeness, but of identity. Man, for instance, is said to be like man, not in essence, but according to property and character; for in essence men are of one nature. And again, man is not said to be unlike dog, but to be of different nature. Accordingly, while the former are of one nature and coessential, the latter are different in both."[3]

2) "In applying to man the being formed into the divine image, we said that man was made in the likeness of his Creator in terms of the quality of his characteristics, habits and the spiritual shape which appears through the beauty of virtues."[4]

Partaking or Participation is when God Shares Some of His Attributes

1) "Therefore, in speaking of 'like' according to essence, we mean like from participation; for 'likeness' is a quality, which may attach to essence, and this would be proper to creatures, for they, by partaking, are made like God. For 'when He shall appear,' says Scripture, 'we shall be like Him', like, that is, not in essence but in sonship, which we shall partake from Him."[5]

2) "We become holy by being conformed to Christ, by partaking of His divine Nature, and by participation in the Holy Spirit."[6]

Sin Caused the Loss of the Image and Likeness of God within Humans

1) "But if, once the transgression had taken off, human beings were now held fast in natural corruption and were deprived of the Grace of being in the image, what else needed to happen?"[7]

2) "He was in the garden, as it is written, still carefully guarding the gift, and was illustrious in the divine image of his Maker through the Holy Spirit who dwelt in him. But when he was led astray by the deception of the devil, he despised the Creator. He trampled on the law that was marked out for him and grieved his Benefactor. The Benefactor took back the Grace that was given to him."[8]

Salvation is the Restoration within Us of Those Things That were Lost

1) Greek etymology: **σωτηρία** = deliverance, preservation > **σωτήρ** = saviour, deliverer > **σώζω** = of things, keep safe, preserve (...) carry off safe, rescue from > **σῶς** = safe and **sound**, alive and well, of persons (...) of things, safe, **whole**.

2) Latin etymology: Salvare = to save > salvus = safe or uninjured; Uninjured means to be **protected from** damage, and damage means **loss** or harm caused by injury.

Illustrations

Practical Means of Salvation, the Restoration of God's Image and Likeness

The Mystical or Sacramental Life

1) Baptism: "the grace of baptism, through which we are all cleansed of all our filth and are declared to be partakers of the divine nature through the Spirit of Christ dwelling in us."[15]
2) Chrismation: "It is when He [the Holy Spirit] is given by the Word that creatures participate in Him."[16]
3) Christ's Body & Blood: "But finally the Bread from heaven, that is, Christ, nourishes us to eternal life both by supplying us with the Holy Spirit and by participation in His own Flesh, placing into us participation with God and destroying death that comes from the ancient Curse."[17]
4) Repentance: "By striving with all our might to do whatever is good and by setting our mind above the pleasures of the flesh, we may preserve intact the beauty of the image that is implanted in us. This is the spiritual life, and this is the meaning of worship in the Spirit."[18]

Specific Tactic for Repentance: Guard the Heart – Watchfulness & Prayer

1) "But because of his likeness to the One who is, which, if he had guarded through his consideration (thinking deeply about) of Him, his natural corruption would have lost its force, he would have remained incorruptible."[19]
2) "Sobriety is a good thing, and guarding our thoughts is extremely profitable, along with the intense desire to do good and to practice virtue. That is how we will work out 'our own salvation.'[20]"[21]
1) "The paths which lead those onward to an uncorrupt life (…) are indeed numerous; but one, which especially benefits those who practice it, is prayer."[22]

Striving to Be a Fellow-Worker with God to Achieve Salvation

1) Is spirituality, the characteristic of being spiritual, for, "being spiritual means that one does not live according to the flesh but rather inclines away from it and toward the will to follow what the Spirit wants."[10]
2) Allows one to actively show love to God, if one's motive is pure, for, "love does not seek its own."[11]
3) Allows one to establish, maintain and grow in a personal relationship with God, for, "we are united to Him through love,"[12] and "in this love the power of our connection or union in the Spirit would be best maintained and preserved;"[13] however, "the person who opts to live without love is not in God, instead lying outside of a relationship with God."[14]

God Wants His Image and Likeness within Us to be Restored

"He [God] desires, then, the nature of humanity to be renewed and reshaped into its original image by partaking of the Spirit so that, by being clothed with that original grace and being restored [into] the shape [that is in conformity with] Him, we may be found superior to and more powerful than sin, which reigns in this world, and we may devote ourselves only to the love of God."[9]

Notes of Illustration 4

1. Athanasius, Against the Heathen. (NPNF² 4), 22.

2. Cyril of Alexandria. (2018–2019). *Glaphyra on the Pentateuch: Genesis, Exodus through Deuteronomy* (N. P. Lunn, Trans.; Vol. 1, p. 70). The Catholic University of America Press.

3. Athanasius, Councils of Ariminum and Seleucia. (NPNF² 4), 478–479.

4. Cyril of Alexandria. (1983). *Answers to Tiberius*. L. Wickham (Trans.), *Cyril of Alexandria: Select letters* (p. 175). Oxford: Oxford University Press.

5. Athanasius, Councils of Ariminum and Seleucia. (NPNF² 4), 478–479.

6. Cyril of Alexandria. Wilken, R. L., Christman, A. R., & Hollerich, M. J., eds. (2007). *Isaiah: Interpreted by Early Christian and Medieval Commentators* (R. L. Wilken, A. R. Christman, & M. J. Hollerich, Trans.; p. 402). William B. Eerdmans Publishing Company.

7. Athanasius the Great of Alexandria. (2011). *On the Incarnation: Translation* (J. Behr, Ed. & Trans.; p. 65). SVS Press.

8. Cyril, Commentary on John, Vol. 1, IVP Academic, 81.

9. Cyril, Commentary on John, Vol. 2, IVP Academic, 297.

10. Cyril of Alexandria. (2022). *Commentaries on Romans, 1-2 Corinthians, and Hebrews* (J. C. Elowsky, G. L. Bray, M. Glerup, & T. C. Oden, Eds.; D. R. Maxwell, Trans.; p. 14). IVP Academic.

11. 1 Cor 13:5.

12. Cyril, Commentary on John, Vol. 2, IVP Academic, 211.

13- Ibid. (Vol. 2, p. 222)

14. Cyril of Alexandria. (2008). *Commentary on the Twelve Prophets*. (T. P. Halton, Ed., R. C. Hill, Trans.) (p. 25). Washington, DC: The Catholic University of America Press.

15. Cyril of Alexandria. (2018–2019). *Glaphyra on the Pentateuch: Genesis, Exodus through Deuteronomy* (N. P. Lunn, Trans.; Vol. 2, p. 197). The Catholic University of America Press.

16. Athanasius and Didymus. (2011). *Works on the Spirit:*

Athanasius's Letters to Serapion on the Holy Spirit, and, Didymus's on the Holy Spirit (J. Behr, Ed.; M. DelCogliano, A. Radde-Gallwitz, & L. Ayres, Trans.; Vol. 43, p. 95). St. Vladimir's Seminary Press.

17. Cyril, Commentary on John, Vol. 1, IVP Academic, 212.

18. Cyril, Commentary on John, Vol. 2, IVP Academic, 297.

19. Athanasius, On the Incarnation of the Word. (NPNF[2] 4), 38.

20. Phi 2:12.

21. Cyril, Commentary on John, Vol. 2, IVP Academic, 289.

22. Cyril of Alexandria. (1859). *A Commentary upon the Gospel according to S. Luke*. (R. P. Smith, Trans.) (p. 551). Oxford: Oxford University Press.

5. The Immediate Goal of Christianity

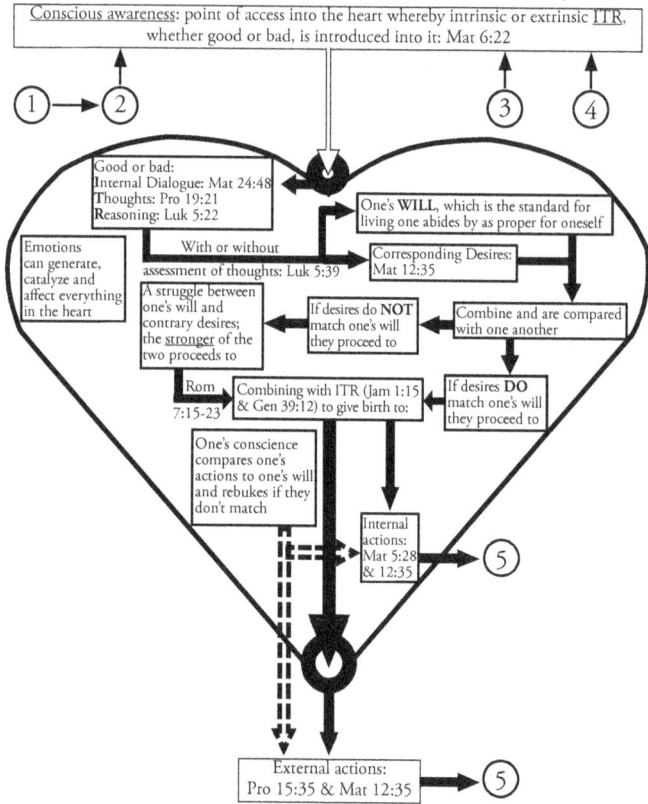

The Immediate Goal of Christianity: Preserving God's Image and Likeness within Us

"By striving with all our might to do whatever is good and by setting our mind above the pleasures of the flesh, we may preserve intact the beauty of the image that is implanted in us. **This is the spiritual life**, and this is the meaning of worship in the Spirit."[1]

"Thus, indeed, the end [goal] of our chosen orientation is eternal life, according to the very words of the Apostle: 'Having your reward, indeed, in holiness, but your end in eternal life.' (…) But the [immediate] goal is purity of heart, which has not undeservedly been called holiness. Without this the aforesaid end will not be able to be seized."[2]

Illustrations

5. The Immediate Goal of Christianity *Cont.*

Conscious awareness: point of access into the heart whereby intrinsic or extrinsic ITR, whether good or bad, is introduced into it: Mat 6:22

(2) Here is the strategic point of resistance; a successful counter-attack here, via **watchfulness**: Mat 13:25, 24:43, Isa 21:6, 26:2-3, Pro 4:22, 15:35, 23:19 & 1The 5:21-22; **humility**: Deu 1:42, Pro 20:19, Amo 2:14, Jer 2:22 & Joh 15:5; & **prayer**: Psa 17:4, 49:15, 55:10, Mat 8:2, 26:41 & 1Joh 1:9, wins the **ENTIRE** war. Abba John said: "I am like somebody sitting beneath a large tree who sees many wild beasts and serpents coming at him. Seeing that he cannot withstand them, he runs up into the tree and is saved. So it is with me I stay in my cell and I see the evil thoughts before me. And when I do not have the strength [to oppose] them, I flee to God in prayer and am saved from the enemy."[6]

(3) We have the ability to and should regulate what type of thoughts enter our hearts: Pro 23:19, Mat 6:22-23, Phi 4:8 & 1The 5:21-22.

(4) **Where the enemy attacks**: Joh 13:2 & Act 5:3.
How the enemy attacks:
1) Plants ungodly ITR: Joh 13:2 & Act 5:3-4.
2) Removes godly ITR: Mar 4:15 & Joh 10:10.
Why the enemy attacks here: Mat 12:35, 13:25, Act 5:4 & Jam 1:15.

Practical Application
1) <u>Prayer</u>: Ask God to teach one how to watch and to keep watch with oneself: Joh 15:5, 1Cor 3:9 & Psa 126:1.
2) <u>Watchfulness</u>: Examine oneself: Psa 76:7, Pro 15:26 & 2Cor 13:5.
3) <u>Humility</u>: accept one's sins which watchfulness reveals: Psa 50:5, 1Tim 1:15 & 1 Joh 1:8.
4) <u>Prayer</u>: Ask God to heal one from these sins: Psa 49:15, 55:10, Mat 8:2-3 & 1Joh 1:9.
5) <u>Watchfulness</u>: Work with God, mentally and/or physically, to keep godly thoughts in and evil ones out: Pro 23:20 & Rom 13:14.

(1) "Examine our own hearts, and try to free them from the passions that dwell within them, and their frailties, by asking it of God: for He it is Who heals the broken in heart, and frees us from the maladies of the soul."[7]

(5)
1) **Striving to keep both good is love**: Pro 15:35, 11:4, Joh 14:21, 23, 1Cor 13:5, 1 Joh 3:17 & 5:3
2) **Love is purity of heart**
"That love whose elements the Apostle describes, which consists in purity of heart alone."[3]
3) **Love is part of existing in God's image and likeness**
"The act [of love] is better than any other kind of well doing [virtue]: for it works in our souls a certain divine likeness which molds us, so to speak, after (into) God's image."[4]
"The boast of love is the face and image of Christ the Savior in us."[5]

---

1. Cyril, Commentary on John, Vol. 2, p. 297.
2. Cassian, The Conferences, p. 44.
3. Ibid. (45).
4. Cyril, Commentary on Luke, pp. 531–532.
5. Cyril, Commentary on John, Vol. 2, p. 141.
6. Behr, J., ed. (2014). *Give Me a Word: The Alphabetical Sayings of the Desert Fathers* (J. Wortley, Trans.; Vol. 52, pp. 133–134). St Vladimir's Seminary Press.
7. Cyril, Commentary on Luke, p. 116.

6. Characteristics of Love

LOVE	
IS:	IS NOT:
Believing of all things (1 Cor 13:7)	Envious (1 Cor 13:4)
Bond of perfection (Col 3:14)	Evil-thinking (1 Cor 13:5)
Corrective (Rev 3:19)	Hypocritical (Rom 12:9)
Edifying (1 Cor 8:1)	Joyful of evil (1 Cor 13:6)
Fruit of the Spirit (Gal 5:22)	Proud (1 Cor 13:4)
Fulfillment of the Law (Rom 13:10 & 2 Jn 1:6)	Provoked (1 Cor 13:5)
Goal of the Law (1 Tim 1:5)	Rude (1 Cor 13:5)
Harmless (Rom 13:10)	Showy (1 Cor 13:4)
Hopeful of all things (1 Cor 13:7)	Self-seeking (1 Cor 13:5)
Kind (1 Cor 13:4)	
Joyful of the truth (1 Cor 13:6)	
Long-suffering (1 Cor 13:4 & 7)	
Painful (Rev 3:19)	
Protective (1 Pet 4:8)	
Self-sacrificial (Jn 15:13 & 1 Cor 13:5)	
Unfailing (1 Cor 13:7 & 8)	

Illustrations

7. Illustration of the Salvific Efficacy of Prayer

Definition of Prayer	Effects of Prayer
Greek Root: Προς- Εὔχομαι. Προς: "expressing direction, on the side of, in the direction of,"[1] Εὔχομαι: "pray for, long or wish for (…) simply, profess or declare."[2] **Patristic Roots:** "True prayer is that which produces the intelligible concept, idea or notion of God in the soul.[3] The dwelling of God in the heart means to have God planted firmly in oneself by memory."[4] "For man to converse with God is a very great honor to human nature. And this we do in prayer."[5] "Well, we define prayer as making a request [to God] for good things, and above all for those things that promote the glory of God and that result in our good conduct and our living a life that is truly pleasing."[6]	**Contemplation[7] of, Encountering, Finding, Meeting, Perceiving or Seeing God** "Then I set my face toward the Lord God to seek[8] Him in prayer and supplication, with fasting, sackcloth, and ashes."[9] **Preservation of God's Image and Likeness within Humanity** "But because of his likeness to the One who is, which, if he had guarded through his consideration (thinking deeply about) of Him, his natural corruption would have lost its force, he would have remained incorruptible."[10] "Ask therefore the bestowal without limitation of spiritual gifts. Ask strength, that you may be able manfully to resist every fleshly lust. Ask of God an uncovetous disposition; long suffering; gentleness; and the mother and nurse of all good, I mean, patience. Ask calmness of temper; self-control; a pure heart; and further, ask also the wisdom that comes from Him. These things He will give readily: these save the soul: these work in it that better beauty, and imprint in it God's image."[11] **Providing of an Opportunity to Love God** "He [God] desires, then, the nature of humanity to be renewed and reshaped into its original image by communion with the Spirit,"[12] and if one pursues restoration of God's image within oneself because one wants to exist the way God wishes one to exist, this constitutes love, because, "love does not seek its own."[13] **Development, Maintenance and Enrichment of a Personal Relationship with God** "So the person who opts to live without love is not in God, instead lying outside of a relationship with God,"[14] for, "we are united to Him through love,"[15] and "in this love the power of our connection or union in the Spirit would be best maintained and preserved."[16] **Equipping of One with a Weapon by which One can Overcome Spiritual Enemies** "Constant and earnest prayer therefore is necessary. For weapons and the tools of warfare are needed for soldiers, that they may be able to overcome those who are drawn up against them: and for us prayer, 'for our weapons,' as Scripture says 'are not carnal, but mighty to God.'[17][8]"[18] "Notice, therefore, how Moses' hands were better than weapons and mounted troops; for as long as he stretched them forth in prayer, Israel was invincible to attack, while if he lowered them, Amalek prevailed."[19]

Notes of Illustration 7

1. Liddell, H. G., Scott, R., Jones, H. S., & McKenzie, R. (1996). In *A Greek-English lexicon* (p. 1496). Clarendon Press.

2. Ibid. (p. 739).

3. Ευχη δε καλη, η εναργη εμποιουσα του Θεου εννοιαν τη ψυχη

4. Basil of Caesarea. (1895). *Letters.* In P. Schaff & H. Wace (Eds.), & B. Jackson (Trans.), *St. Basil: Letters and Select Works* (Vol. 8, p. 111). Christian Literature Company.

5. Cyril, Commentary on Luke, p. 357.

6. Cyril of Alexandria. (2022). *Commentaries on Romans, 1-2 Corinthians, and Hebrews* (J. C. Elowsky, G. L. Bray, M. Glerup, & T. C. Oden, Eds.; D. R. Maxwell, Trans.; p. 23). IVP Academic.

7. θεωρία: "viewing, beholding (…) of the mind, contemplation, consideration;" Liddell, p. 797.

8. εὑρεῖν. Infinitive form εὑρίσκω: "Find (…) find or get for oneself"; Liddell, p. 729. STRONG'S NUMBER: g2147: "find, get, meet with, obtain, perceive or see."

9. Dan. 9:3 LXX (OSB).

10. Athanasius the Great of Alexandria. (2011). *On the Incarnation: Translation* (J. Behr, Ed. & Trans.; p. 59). SVS Press.

11. Cyril, Commentary on Luke, p. 361.

12. Cyril, Commentary on John. Vol. 2, p. 297.

13. 1 Cor 13:5.

14. Cyril of Alexandria. (2008). *Commentary on the Twelve Prophets.* (T. P. Halton, Ed., R. C. Hill, Trans.) (Vol. 116, p. 25). Washington, DC: The Catholic University of America Press.

15. Cyril, Commentary on John. Vol. 2, p. 211.

16. Ibid., Vol. 2, p. 222.

17. 2 Cor 10:4.

18. Cyril, Commentary on Luke, pp. 356–357.

19. Cyril of Alexandria. (2013). *Festal Letters, 13–30* (J. J. O'Keefe & D. G. Hunter, Eds.; P. R. Amidon, Trans.; Vol. 127, p. 80). The Catholic University of America Press.

Bibliography

Athanasius of Alexandria. (1892). In P. Schaff & H. Wace, eds. *St. Athanasius: Select Works and Letters* (Vol. 4). Christian Literature Company.

Athanasius the Great of Alexandria. (2011). *On the Incarnation: Translation* (J. Behr, Ed. & Trans.; Vol. 44a). St. Vladimir's Seminary Press.

Athanasius and Didymus. (2011). *Works on the Spirit: Athanasius's Letters to Serapion on the Holy Spirit, and, Didymus's on the Holy Spirit* (J. Behr, Ed.; M. DelCogliano, A. Radde-Gallwitz, & L. Ayres, Trans.; Vol. 43). St. Vladimir's Seminary Press.

Basil of Caesarea. (1895). In P. Schaff & H. Wace, eds. *St. Basil: Letters and Select Works* (Vol. 8). Christian Literature Company.

Cyril of Alexandria. (1859). *A Commentary upon the Gospel according to S. Luke*. R. P. Smith, trans. Oxford University Press.

Cyril of Alexandria. (1881). *Five Tomes against Nestorius; Scholia on the Incarnation; Christ Is One; Fragments against Diodore of Tarsus,*

Theodore of Mopsuestia, the Synousiasts. James Parker and Co.; Rivingtons.

Cyril of Alexandria. (1983). *Cyril of Alexandria: Select letters*. L. Wickham, trans. Oxford: Oxford University Press.

Cyril of Alexandria. (1987). *Letters, 51–110*. T. P. Halton, ed.; J. I. McEnerney, trans. The Catholic University of America Press.

Cyril of Alexandria. (2002). *Matthew 14–28*. M. Simonetti, ed. InterVarsity Press.

Cyril of Alexandria. (2008). *Commentary on Isaiah*. R. C. Hill, trans. Holy Cross Orthodox Press.

Cyril of Alexandria. (2008). *Commentary on the Twelve Prophets*. T. P. Halton, ed.; R. C. Hill, trans. The Catholic University of America Press.

Cyril of Alexandria. (2009). *Festal Letters, 1–12*. J. J. O'Keefe, ed.; P. R. Amidon, trans. The Catholic University of America Press.

Cyril of Alexandria. (2013–2015). *Commentary on John*, 2 volumes. J. C. Elowsky, T. C. Oden, & G. L. Bray, eds.; D. R. Maxwell, trans. Downers Grove, IL: IVP Academic: An Imprint of InterVarsity Press.

Cyril of Alexandria. (2018–2019). *Glaphyra on the Pentateuch: Genesis, Exodus through Deuteronomy*, 2 volumes. N. P. Lunn, trans. The Catholic University of America Press.

Cyril of Alexandria. (2021). *On Veneration and Worship in Spirit and Truth: Book Nine*. J. Gohl, trans.

Cyril of Alexandria. (2022). *Commentaries on Romans, 1-2 Corinthians, and Hebrews*. J. C. Elowsky, G. L. Bray, M. Glerup, & T. C. Oden, eds.; D. R. Maxwell, trans. IVP Academic: An Imprint of InterVarsity Press.

Cyril of Alexandria. (2023). *Thesaurus of the Holy and Consubstantial Trinity*. J. Tomes & M. Garcia, trans. Greystone Theological Institute.

John Cassian. (1997). *John Cassian: The Conferences*. W. J. Burghardt, J. Dillon, & D. D. McManus, eds.; B. Ramsey, trans. Newman Press.

Letters of Ammonas, Chitty D., trans. (Oxford: Sisters of the Love of God, 1979). Letter 10.

Liddell H. G., Scott R., Jones H. S., & McKenzie R. (1996). In *A Greek-English lexicon*. Clarendon Press.

Mark the Monk. (2009). *Counsels on the Spiritual Life*. J. Behr, ed.; T. Vivian & A. Casiday, trans. St. Vladimir's Seminary Press.

Saint Macarius the Spiritbearer. (2004). *Saint Macarius the Spiritbearer: Coptic Texts Relating to Saint Macarius the Great*. J. Behr, ed.; T. Vivian, trans. St. Vladimir's Seminary Press.

The Book of the Elders: Sayings of the Desert Fathers

- *The Systematic Collection*, Wortley J., trans. (Collegeville: Liturgical Press, 2012), 15.100.

The Sayings of the Desert Fathers: The Alphabetical Collection, Ward B., trans. (Kalamazoo: Cistercian Publications, 1975).

www.ingramcontent.com/pod-product-compliance
Lightning Source LLC
Chambersburg PA
CBHW031410040426
42444CB00005B/504